William Henry Abbott, Frederick F. Wyman

Lyrics and Lays

William Henry Abbott, Frederick F. Wyman

Lyrics and Lays

ISBN/EAN: 9783744776134

Printed in Europe, USA, Canada, Australia, Japan

Cover: Foto ©Thomas Meinert / pixelio.de

More available books at **www.hansebooks.com**

LYRICS AND LAYS.

BY

PIPS.

CALCUTTA :
PUBLISHED BY WYMAN BROS., HARE STREET.

1867.

Dedicated to

THE COMFORT OF MY LIFE OF TOIL,
MY TREASURED LITTLE WIFE.

CONTENTS.

INEVITABLE PREFACE.

THE Printers have told me positively that this book cannot be published without a Preface. I beg therefore, by way of Preface, to state that these effusions of mine have been collected from the "Englishman," the "Indian Daily News," the "Indian Freemason's Friend," the "Oriental Sporting Magazine," and a scrapbook of my own. I know that some of the so-called squibs have created a smile on many a friend's face, even during the *ennui* of an Indian hot weather. If they do so again, I shall be well rewarded for the trouble which their collection and revision have given me.

Calcutta, May 1867.

LYRICS AND LAYS,

BY

PIPS.

THE TRIPLE SELL.

IN 1849, Lord Gough, then Commander-in-Chief in India, was about to retire from the command, and Sir William Gomm, who was at the Mauritius, had already been nominated to succeed him, when the second Sikh Campaign broke out and Lord Gough took the field once more. He was all but defeated at Moodkee, Ferozeshur, and Chillianwallah. The public outcry at home for the immediate despatch of Sir Charles Napier to relieve Lord Gough was so great that the Court of Directors reluctantly sent him out. But Lord Gough fought and won the battle of Guzerat, which completely put an end to the campaign, and Sir Charles Napier came out too late and had to go back again. When Sir William Gomm arrived he found that Sir Charles had been sent for, and he too was sold; eventually he was confirmed in the appointment.

𝔓𝔞𝔯𝔱 𝔦.

The Court of Directors in old Leadenhall,
  With visages grim and pale,
Have met to discuss what has troubled them all,
  The news by the Overland Mail.

How the fiery Gough had been silly enough
    To get fierce at a single shot,
And a jungle thick with his men to stuff,
    Where the fire was frightfully hot.

How the Sikhs mow'd down our men like grass,
    How some of our men ran away,
How the great "Cold Stayle" behaved like an ass,
    On Chillianwallah's sad day.

"Now listen, my friends," said their Chairman grave,
    "This news is dismal enough;
"Oh! where shall we find a veteran brave
    "To take the command from old Gough?

"An awful official I hold in my hand
    "From that obstinate pig-headed Duke,
"Which begins uncommonly like a command
    "And finishes with rebuke.

"It commands us to India old Charlie to send
    "To fight out this wretched campaign;
"We long ago made of the old man an end—
    "We surely won't have him again.

" Another good soldier there needs must be
  " In England's army true,
" If not much better as good as he
  " Who in this sore trouble will do."

Then loud did they bawl, the Directors all,
  " The Duke shall not interfere ;
" We're the rulers of India in old Leadenhall,
  " We'll have none of the Napiers here."

But their wrath and fuming were all in vain,
  For all, throughout England, cried,
" Send out old Charlie to India again
  " Ere worse luck us betide."

And so the Directors did eat their leek
  And swallow most humble pie,
And they order'd old Charlie within the week
  Again to the wars to hie.

Sir Charles Napier was fond of a fight
  Altho' an old man was he,
And he laugh'd and he cried with great delight—
  Once more in arms to be.

" Now where is my page so bold," quoth he,
  " And where is my portmanteau ?
" Now pack me a shirt and some soap and see
  " How soon the ' Ripon ' will go."

Again to the wars this aged knight
    Rush'd off with boyish glee,
And, oh, 'twas a goodly pleasant sight
    The curl of his beard to see.

Full many a night, full many a day,
    Full many a week and more,
Pass'd by ere the anxious warrior stept
    Again upon India's shore.

And when he arrived how he cursed his fate,
    He tore his hair outright,
The Sikhs had been thrash'd, he was all too late
    For anything like a fight.

But cursing his fate was useless now,
    And tearing his hair all vain,
He came to India to share in the row
    But—had to go back again !

And thus the warrior himself was sold,
    And the Court of Directors too—
They felt that they had been sadly cajoled,
    And he had found nothing to do.

𝕻𝖆𝖗𝖙 2.

CHILLIANWALLAH.

Night closes o'er the battle plain
Where hundreds of unburied slain
   Are stretched in bloody groups,
And those who ne'er will fight again
Throughout that silent ghastly train
   Are mostly British troops.

And 'mid the camp-fire's lurid glare
With voice suppress'd, with sullen air,
   Long through the weary night,
The worn survivors deeply swear
At him whose folly led them where
   They had no chance to fight.

And to and fro before his tent,
His rage all gone, his fury spent,
   Lord Gough doth slowly pace;
Deep shame and anguish both are blent
In every line and lineament
   Of the old warrior's face.

Well may he gaze thro' mist and rain
To where the Sikhs their camp maintain,
  And think on what he has done;
The whole day long he has fought in vain,
The Sikhs have got their guns again,
  Alas! what has he won?

That morning with the dawn of light
He suddenly had come in sight
  Of thirty thousand Sikhs,
And burning for the coming fight
His heart beat high with fierce delight,
  And flush'd his florid cheeks.

At once he mark'd his plan of attack
When the Sikhs sent a shot across his track,
  Close to his startled horse;
Of patience Lord Gough had a dreadful lack,
He gave the word to lead on in a crack
  The whole of the British force.

How Chillianwallah's fight was fought,
And how Lord Gough great wonders wrought,
  And how he spiked a gun,
How bitter a lesson that Lord was taught,
How instead of Shere Singh a Tartar he caught,
  Are known to every one.

So leave him at the great tent door,
And let him there his loss deplore,
  For he avenged it well.
He played the Irish fool no more,
And well he kept the oath he swore
  That night the Sikhs to sell.

GUZERAT.

Now turn we to another strain
  And to another fight,
And write in far more pleasant vein
  Of a more pleasant sight.

'Twas morn, and scarce the god of day
  Had tipp'd the clouds with gold,
When bugle call and trumpet bray
  Of coming battle told.

Old Chutter Singh had join'd his son,
  And Whish had join'd Lord Gough ;
The odds were then full ten to one,
  The Sikhs would have enough.

For quiet was Lord Gough that day,
  He kept the oath he swore,
That at long bowls he'd blaze away
  Until the fight was o'er.

Ah! turn ye, turn ye, Sikhs so bold,
    Ah! turn you, Chutter Singh,
Or else you surely will be sold
    For all your blustering.

Four times did charge the Afghan horse,
    With shouts and gestures dire,
And four times turn'd they in mid course,
    They relish'd not the fire.

For such a storm of round and grape
    Pour'd from the British side,
That no one could that storm escape
    Who did not quickly ride.

And when but three short hours had pass'd,
    Lord Gough was fairly dazed
To see the Sikhs had fired their last,
    Their guns no longer blazed.

Then cried he, " Let our line advance
    " And strike the final blow,
" Each Lancer forward with his lance
    " To spear the flying foe."

And as Shere Singh perceived the line
    Advancing thro' the smoke,
He said " By Allah, this is fine,
    " But ah! it is no joke."

His governor was standing by,
    And to him turned his son;
" Now governor, let you and I
    " Like blazes cut and run."

Woe, woe, unto the Sikhs that day;
    You could not count the slain,
Or those who badly wounded lay
    Upon that bloody plain.

Thus Hugh Lord Gough did sell the Sikhs
    And all the world beside,
And no one for his former tricks
    That lord does now deride.

Part 3.

SIR WILLIAM GOMM.

There was a knight of great renown, a soldier brave
    was he,
Altho' he never had the luck a single fight to see.
The only war-note he had heard was beat of evening
    drum,
Or bugle call upon parade; his name was William
    Gomm.

This knight had been the Governor of famed Mauritius
    Isle,
And well we know he govern'd there in very brilliant
    style;
His reign of course expired with the usual term of years,
And he gave up the government in silence and in tears.

And, oh! throughout the Isle of France what grief
    was in each heart,
With such a fine old Governor to think that they must
    part;
And old and young thus murmur'd there in sad and
    mournful strain,
" When will this Island ever have such a Governor
    again ?"

But all such pain is ever vain when hostile fates decree
The Governor and the govern'd henceforth must parted be.
So the men soon gave up murmuring, the women dried
    their eyes,
And pleasant smiles and laughter took the place of tears
    and sighs.

And Sir William was appointed, to his very great relief,
To the post he long had sigh'd for, the Indian Army's
    Chief;
Ah! thankfully he read the letter that order'd him to
    start,
And the gentle hint from Government to look a little
    smart.

"Now run my page and quickly see what ship will soon-
  est go
And in the twinkling of an eye come back and let me
  know,
For in this little Island I may no longer stay,
Now go at once and see what ship will first be under
  weigh."

*   *   *   *   *   *

Glorious has the sun gone down
    To his golden rest,
Darker shadows have been thrown
    Over ocean's breast.

Gently sighs the evening breeze,
    Fall the dews of night,
Glides yon vessel through the seas
    In the calm moonlight.

On her deck Sir William Gomm
    Takes his evening cheer,
Thinking of the time to come
    And his past career;

Happy in the pleasing dream
    Of his appointment good,
Truly doth Sir William seem
    In a pleasant mood.

The proverb he hath quite forgot,
   A proverb all unmatch'd,
"To count his chicks a man ought not
   Till they all are hatch'd."

    *   *   *.   *   *   *

Another barque is sailing o'er that tranquil moonlit sea
And coming up is rounded to under the stranger's lee ;
A boat soon lower'd from her side comes dancing o'er
   the wave
And takes on board the stranger, the Pilot stern and
   grave.

No sooner is his foot on deck than all about him crowd
And for the chief and latest news each one doth question loud.
"Now tell us, honest Pilot, all the news that you have
   brought,
"How goes that dreadful Sikh campaign, what battles
   have been fought ?"

And to such questions adds the knight with conscious
   pride and glee
"The Commander-in-Chief of India in me, my friend,
   you see !"
"Now noble Sir," the Pilot said, "you surely do not
   know
" Of what at home did happen but a little while ago,

"How the aged Charlie Napier all England did select
"To fill that fine appointment which you yourself
expect."
"Ah me! ah me! can this be true? Oh! Pilot say not so,
"Oh! never on myself before did fall so sad a blow."

It was indeed alas too true Sir William Gomm did find,
And grief and bitter rage now fill'd his lately happy
mind.
He raved and storm'd at every one and like old Charlie
swore,
He smote his hand upon his breast, his hair he wildly
tore.

And thus Sir William Gomm was sold, his Aides-de-
camp the same,
Who came here on his staff in hopes to reap renown and
fame;
And 'tis a pleasant task for me, far more than I can tell,
To close this last and saddest part of this thrice dismal sell.

THE MASONIC DINNER.

On the laying of the foundation stone of the Calcutta Fever Hospital in 1848, the Governor General, then Lord Dalhousie, a great mason, was present as a guest.

Begirt with many a brother true
    Apparel'd in masonic dress,
The Pro. Grand Master's looks were blue
    And something on his mind did press.

Bright shone the jewels of his rank,
    His collar, apron, both were new,
But something made his face seem blank,
    And all remark'd that G — t look'd blue.

"Why looks he so?" each one did ask,
    And ever thus the answer ran,
"He has this night the awful task
    Of entertaining a great man."

Aye, the greatest man in all the land
    Had come to join the masons' board,
To take each humble brother's hand
    And in the mason drop the lord.

The brethren are met in the old Town Hall
And gaily their banners hang out from each wall,
Those banners whose symbols such secrecy lend
With flags of all nations mysteriously blend,
And twined round the pillars with exquisite care
Are the compasses, gavel, gauge, chisel, and square,—
The All-seeing Eye and the man in the moon
And the cock that wakes masons a great deal too soon,
While double triangles, with trowel and hod,
And skull and cross-bones look decidedly odd.
And now every brother sits down in his place
With an air of deep mystery over his face.
Dark-blue and gold collars are worn by the swells
While light-blue and silver of lower rank tells.
(Those colours so loved after wearisome cram,
The dark-blue of Isis, the light-blue of Cam).
The Provincial Grand Master presides at the board,
On his right sits the guest of the evening, a lord,
A real live lord come to dine with the craft!
The thought almost drives the poor Grand Master daft!
On his left sits old Longuey, a Nestor of law,
And ever midst masons a real Bashaw!
The dishes are lifted, the dinner begun,
The dinner is eaten, the dinner is done.
But the poor P. G. M. remains hungry and blue
He has found in kow-towing far too much to do.

"Sub nukkur bar jagga" C—e wrathfully cries
With a twist of his lips and the fire in his eyes,
" Sub nukkur bar jagga" he screams out again,
His face as distorted as if 'twere in pain.
They hear him at last and they all disappear,
And the hall from one end to the other is clear.

The Provincial Grand Master
    Gets up from his chair,
His blood runs the faster
    From being chief there.

Before a great Earl
    A great speech he must make,
His head's in a whirl,
    So a peg he must take ;

Dutch courage at last
    Gives him strength to proceed,
And though he spoke fast
    'Twas a sad speech indeed !

But before he spoke his eyes were shock'd
At a sight which all his senses mock'd—
Three ignorant brethren, sad to record,
Were smoking their hookahs before a lord ! ! !
" And who dares to smoke in a presence so great,
" Who so presumptuous an Earl thus to treat ?

" What ignorant brethren have brought hookahs here?
" They surely have taken too freely of beer?
" Away, away, take those hookahs away,
" And let them be seen here no more to-day."
And turning to Earl D—e he said—
" Most noble Earl, not on my poor head
" Let this fault be visited, no, not on me,
" 'Tis the ignorant only who smoke before thee!"

And now for his speech which was truly absurd,
Such a long string of humbug was ne'er before heard:—
" Most noble, most great, most illustrious man,
" I rise in your honour, to speak if I can,
" But thou art too lordly, too noble of birth,
" My poor humble praises can ne'er tell your worth,
" Myself and my brethren, oh, wonderful lord,
" Have invited you here to our poor humble board.
" Oh, how shall we thank the great man that has given
" Such joy to our hearts and made this hall a heaven?
" What pleasure, what rapture, what exquisite pride,
" To be called by you brother and sit by your side!
" Ah! would my poor tongue, now so feeble, could say
" All my own heart has felt on this glorious day.
" Of all Indian G. G.'s that I can recall,
" Thou, most noble Dalhousie, art head of them all.
" The noble Lord Hastings I'll first call to mind,
" And the number of friends that he left behind;

"Then Bentinck, the wise, the impartial, the good—

"The honest Lord Auckland so gentle of mood,

"I remember the mild and benignant old Bird,

"(Of the fate of whose portrait, my Lord, you have
    heard)

"The gallant Lord Ellenborough, fearless and free,

"I speak well of him—he was patron to me;

"Then the brave warrior Hardinge, whose final campaign

"Must, alas, for poor India, be fought o'er again;

"The orator Pearson, the lynx-eyed and grave,

"And (in naming another your patience I crave—

"For in naming him now my long list I have done)

"The illustrious Maddock who's now in Ceylon.

"Ah! wonderful Earl, before you they all fade,

"And their greatness and goodness are cast in the
    shade,

"When I think of the eloquent speech which you gave

"When we all met to honor the gallant and brave,

"Oh, I feel, noble Earl, I could now bend the knee,

"And pour out my praises to thee, Earl, to thee.

"Now, brethren, the toast: up, up on your legs,

"A bumper let each brother drain to the dregs.

"'Here's a health to our good noble guest of to-night,

"'The great Earl and brother who sits at my right.'"

The speech, alas, was hissed, but the toast was well
    received,

Though bitterly the brethren for their Grand Master
    grieved;

They felt that in Dalhousie's eyes the craft was sadly
 lower'd
By all the butter and the oil which on him had been
 shower'd.

*   *   *   *   *

Here the manuscript in verse ceases; it must therefore be added
that Lord Dalhousie's reply was as good as the speech of the Provincial
Grand Master was feeble, and was, sentence by sentence, rapturously
applauded, and when, pleading weakness of body and cares of State,
Lord Dalhousie gave the toast—

" To Masons' wives and Masons' bairns
" And all who hang on Masons' arms"—

and then retired, the heart of every one there went with Andrew
Ramsay, Earl of Dalhousie.

October, 1848.

THE MUSK-RAT AND PLANTER.

A tale of facts which happened in Bengal in 1850, and formed a practical exposition of Act XVIII of that year.

A Musk-rat once, of great renown,
Ruled o'er a little country town,
His want of sense, his pride of place,
Shewed him the dullest of his race.
So fond of rambling out at night,
He knew not what was wrong or right.
In one small way he did excel—
He played the tom-tom very well;
And neighbours have been heard to say,
As soon as day to night gave way,
He through the city would parade
And treat them to a serenade.

Music, by all it is confess'd,
Hath charms to soothe the savage breast:
And when that music, soft and clear,
Comes stealing on the listening ear;
When on some lovely summer night
The moon above is shining bright

And rivals daylight with her glare,
When not a sound disturbs the air,
And when the mind and soul are given
To thoughts that only breathe of heaven,—
Then when in cadence soft and low
Some melody of long ago
Comes gently whispering on the ear,—
Oh! music's strains are then most dear.

But when in some secluded spot
Where nights as well as days are hot,
Some silly fool, to whom kind heaven
An ear for music has not given,
Who fancies that the noisy beat
Of common tom-tom must be sweet,
And promenades the streets at night
And bangs away with all his might,
When weary wretches, roused from sleep,
Launch at him curses loud and deep,
For breaking up their quiet rest,
And when that noisy dreadful pest
To worry them bangs more and more,—
Then music is an awful bore.

And thus it chanced not long ago,
This Musk-rat would tom-tomming go;
And one dark night, tom-tom in hand,
He led his bajah-wallah band—

A dirty, filthy, screaming crew—
Who every step more noisy grew,
To where a neighbouring Planter dwelt,
For whom Musk-rat no liking felt.
With shouts and cries, tom-tom in hand,
He led his wild unruly band
To where the Planter's dwelling stood,
And thus addressed his noisy brood :
"My friends, there dwells a Planter here
" Who ever greets me with a sneer,
" Who being from my rule exempt
" Doth ever treat me with contempt ;
" And now (he added, with a frown)
" This Planter's pride I will take down ;
" Come batter down his compound gate,
" And then his house illuminate."
He said : and soon, the work begun,
The gate was forced, the house was won,
And mid a wild and deafening din
The bajah-wallahs all rushed in.
Loud yelled the bajah-wallahs then,
Bang, bang, the tom-toms went again,
And in that dread discordant sound
The Planter's feeble voice was drowned ;
And bang went crackers, squibs, in scores,
Shot through the windows and the doors,

And Catherine wheels went spinning round,
And Roman candles strewed the ground;
Tables and chairs were tossed about—
The lower floor turned inside out:
And midst the din the Planter's wife
Was soon in terror of her life;
She and her daughters, all undressed,
Into the midst had wildly pressed,
But finding shrieks and tears were vain,
They ran up to their rooms again.
The Planter through the back-gate made
His own escape to call for aid.
Then Musk-rat fled, for well he knew
He could not long restrain his crew,
And with one farewell rattling bang,
And with a yell whose echoes rang
Far o'er the plain he march'd away,
Making his bajah-wallahs play
The air that he had learnt at home—
" See me, the conquering hero, come. "
The Planter with some friends return'd
Who all for vengeance fiercely burn'd;
But 'twas too late—Musk-rat had fled,
And by this time was safe in bed.
Then loud and long the Planter swore
Such pranks Musk-rat should play no more;

That he himself the following day
Would to a Justice make his way,
And to his Worship get access,
Explain his wrongs and beg redress :
And thus resolved, with anger fired,
The Planter to his bed retired.

The morning came, the Planter rose,
His ire not soften'd by repose ;
And, all impatient of delay,
He to the Town Court took his way,
Where, ' axe' in hand and full of thought,
An ancient Counsellor held his Court,
And who, for wisdom, deep, profound,
Through all the country was renown'd ;
And who, so say they at that place,
Before deciding on a case,
And to avoid unjust attacks,
Would frequently consult his 'axe,'
Which oftentimes a handle gave
The Counsellor's good name to save.
This axe was very sharp and bright
Although it was not always right,
And what was much more to its praise,
It could, when wanted, cut both ways.
The Court was clear'd, the Planter heard,
He told the Counsellor word for word

Of what took place the night before,
And how he soon expected more
Of Musk-rat's tyranny, unless
The Court would give him prompt redress.
The Counsellor heard the story through
And gave it all attention due;
Then order'd that Musk-rat be brought
Without delay into the Court.
His servants scour'd the country round,
And in a trice Musk-rat was found
And brought into the Court with speed
There in his own defence to plead.

The Counsellor spoke—" Pray what defence
Have you for all this violence ?"
The Musk-rat answer'd with a sneer,
" Act Eighteen of the present year."
The Planter said " You must be crack'd
" To take defence upon an Act;
" Into a private house to take
" A mob of madmen and to break
" The whole house down. Oh, Musk-rat, fie,
" Such deeds no Act will justify."
Musk-rat then boldly spoke again
" Sir Counsellor, 'tis very plain
" I and the Planter can't agree,
" You must decide 'twixt him and me ;

" I for my part of course abide
" By what your bright axe* may decide,
" For though you may my statements doubt,
" I acted in good faith throughout."
The Counsellor was nothing loth
And thus it was agreed by both.
So turning to his axe he said :
" Come, bring your judgment to our aid,
" You've heard the Planter's story through,
" And Musk-rat can't deny 'tis true,
" Now, on this subject, what say you ?"
The axe upon its handle rose
And turning on the angry foes,
He to them all in turns display'd
Each side of his bright shining blade,
When, lo, on each side did appear
In glittering letters bright and clear
The following judgment which reveal'd
How dreadfully that axe was steel'd
Against the Planter's humble prayer
That justice might be shewn him there,
And these the words. " The case is clear,
" Redress the Planter can't have here ;

---

* *Axe*, a bundle or volume of *Acts*.

" For though his case is very strong,
" And Musk-rat did him grievous wrong,
" Yet have they both appeal'd to me,
" And I by law must guided be;
" Act eighteen-hundred-fifty rules
" That to protect judicial fools
" And give them every chance to escape
" When they may get into a scrape,
" If they will swear, though false no doubt,
" They acted in good faith throughout,
" They shall from punishment be free
" And 'gainst complaints protected be.
" This Musk-rat swears; and I am bound
" The law in this case to expound,
" Thus, tyranny is back'd by might,
" The farmer's wrong, Musk-rat is right."

Then spoke the Counsellor to the two,
" The judgment has been read by you,
" Now go, I've nothing more to say,
" I've had enough to do to-day."
Then went they forth, but at the door
The Planter many a curse did pour
Upon Musk-rat's devoted head
And with an oath of vengeance said :
" May wither'd hopes my future blast,
" If I don't pay you off at last;

" What shall prevent my vengeance due
" From bringing misery on you?"
The Musk-rat answer'd with a sneer,
" Act 18 *of the present year.*"

MORAL.

Now Planters all, both great and small,
    Attend unto my moral;
If near Civilians you do live,
    Don't with them pick a quarrel,

However cautious you may be,
    However good and thrifty,
You may have reason soon to curse
    The Act 18 of fifty;

But if you're forced into a row
    And cannot do without it,
Take my advice and fight it out,
    Don't go to law about it,

And when a man into your house
    Will *vi et armis* enter
And set the place on fire, why, then
    Pitch *him* into the centre.

THE SONG OF EL BLASÉ.

The sun has sunk below the sea, the breeze has died away,
The restless waves are bright beneath with phosphores-
 cent ray,
And scarce a sound disturbs the air except the distant
 roar
Of the breakers as they dash upon the reefs along the
 shore.

And as I tread the silent deck I think of former years,
And memory now recalls to me my youthful hopes and
 fears;
I think, if all my later joys and griefs could come again,
How little those would pleasure me, how sadly these
 would pain.

In early life, when quite a boy, I left the dear old home
Where never since has fate allow'd my longing steps
 to roam;
Where the only thoughts that troubled me were of the
 happy past,
I did not think the future could with clouds be overcast.

Ah me! and why does memory bring that long ago
    to me,
It only tells me what I was and what I ne'er can be;
My friends are gone, my hopes are fled, alas! I only feel
The man what would get on in life must have a heart
    of steel.

I think how few the real friends I now and then have seen,
Since on the rough world's thorny paths a traveller
    I've been.
And where are those few friends I had? Some gone
    away, some dead,
And none remain to comfort now and cheer me in
    their stead.

I think on all the fairy forms on which I've loved to gaze,
Whose smiles I often long'd for through many weary
    days;
I see them now as then I should before they won my love,
The silly, trifling, jilting things that women ever prove.

And pondering thus, what wonder then my heart should
    seem so cold,
And be no more the trusty heart it used to be of old?
Tho' young, I feel my nature changed, the world has
    closed above
The little stock that nature had of goodness, truth, and
    love.

Oh ! would I ne'er could think upon those early happy
  years
Before my boyhood's fleeting griefs gave way to real
  tears ;
They only serve with greater force the truth to call to,
  mind,
" We leave, in leaving childhood's shores, life's fairy land
  behind."

THE CHEE-CHEE BALL.

The Chee-Chees held high festival in old Domingo's Hall,
And I was there, tho' I was not invited to the ball;
But they receiv'd me kindly, all owing, as I trust,
To my appearance proving me one of the "upper
    crust."

And merrily I pass'd the time, although 'twas somewhat
    slow—
I danced like mad each polka, with lots of heel and toe:
For Chee-Chees think that polkas are very like Scotch
    reels,
And that to dance them properly you must kick up your
    heels.

And there was one, a petite belle, a modest little girl,
Her hair was twisted down her cheeks in many a spiral
    curl;
Her teeth were polish'd ivory, her eyes were very bright,
And the little thing look'd blacker from being dress'd
    in white.

And ever as I saw this girl I mark'd a little man
Whom lovingly she ogled behind her prettty fan :
They always danced together, or, as far as I could see,
When they couldn't dance together they stood up
    vis-a-vis.

'Twas clear they were affianced, that very happy pair,
They seem'd to think themselves to be the only couple
    there ;
And so they whiled away the time till dinner was
    announced—
Oh ! how quickly at that word all through the doorway
    bounced.

Alas ! for some poor hungry ones the supper-room was
    small,
And the company was numerous, it couldn't hold them all ;
So while the few and lucky ones were eating stews and
    grills,
The others kept their hunger down with polkas and
    quadrilles.

Now while the supper disappear'd, I sought for fresher air,
My nose 'mid Kentish hop-grounds rear'd is not the
    nose to bear.
The scent of oil of cocoanut with that of bad perfume,
And the odour of hot dishes in a densely crowded room.

And while I stroll'd alone outside I started at the sound
Of whispering voices near me—I turn'd and gazed
    around;
Yes, there they were, that happy pair, their steps they
    slowly traced,
Her arm was on his shoulder, and his was round her waist;

And, wandering by thus lovingly, their words· fell on
    my ear,—
For he had slightly raised his voice, not thinking I was
    near,
And the very moon look'd clearer, and brighter shone
    each star,—
As the little man imploringly said " Betsy, bolo hah !"

I turn'd and quickly left the spot, I did not like to stay,
To be, as I must else have been, in those two lovers' way;
(To spoil such sport has ever been from my intention far)
And as I walk'd away I heard her gently murmur
    " Hah."

The dance was o'er; before I left, I found myself once more
Close to that happy Chee-Chee pair outside Domingo's
    door;
What pass'd between them I can't say, but those who
    wish to know,
May judge from what I heard, which was " Our ekto
    kissee do."

THE BOXWALLAH,

OR

THE EASTERN KNIGHT OF TOGGENBURG.

— —   —

" Mem Saheb, a Boxwallah's love
  Gives my things to thee,
Though their value's far above
  What thou givest to me.
Kindly couldst thou treat me now
  To one little kiss,
Such as Hindoo girls allow—
  Bapree! what is this?"

Madly jump'd she from her chair,
  To her feet she sprung,
Box'd his ears upon the stair,
  Box'd them till they wrung.
" Go you wretch, you nasty soor;"
  And he bolted straight
Down the staircase, through the door,
  Through the compound gate.

High your prices, good your things,
　　Hero of the box,
But thy heart her treatment wrings,
　　As thine ears her knocks.
Rivaller of Bodelio,
　　Boudet and Gervain,
How thy heart is heavy, oh,
　　How thine ears do pain.

Heavy is the poor man's box
　　Which his cooly bears,
Full of babies' things and frocks
　　Such as childhood wears.
Ee-silk, ee-satin, u-dek-lone,
　　Ebery ting he got,
But his happiness is gone,
　　Weary is his lot.

Back to the bazaar he went,
　　There he shut up shop,
To his home his steps he bent,
　　For he could not stop
In the place where men had seen
　　Him so sadly used,
In the place where he had been
　　Beaten and abused.

In his native village where
   Waves a Cocoanut,
In the drainy, smoky air
   O'er a dirty hut,
Dwells the poor man for a while
   Gorging maunds of rice,
Full of rage and full of bile
   Spending all his pice.

Then his savings nearly gone
   Once more home he left,
Tired of living all alone
   And of hope bereft ;
Longing once again to be
   Where his eyes can trace,
Where they now and then may see,
   That dear form and face.

So one evening very late,
   Footsore, weary, lame,
To the lady's well known gate
   Once again he came,
And the Durwan at the door
   On him fierce did look,
Not the same man who before
   Large dustoorie took.

Then he put a bright rupee
  In the Durwan's palm,
Well he knew that coin would be
  Like Columbian balm,
Saying, " Where's that lady who
  Here last year did dwell,
A Houri with such eyes as you
  See in a Gazelle?"

Low the Durwan then replied,
  " She whom now you seek
" Lately has become a bride,
  " Married just a week,
" And she's now at Alipore
  " Fairest of the fair,
" With the same dark eyes of yore
  " And the same black hair."

Soon he found her dwelling-place,
  Soon he saw her there,
And he gazed upon her face
  With a longing stare ;
And he took a little hut
  Opposite her gate,
Cover'd o'er with dust and soot
  In a wretched state.

There he chew'd whole seers of pawn
  While his beard he stroked,
And all day, a wretch forlorn,
  Hubble-bubble smoked.
When, a passing glimpse allow'd,
  She rode happy by,
To the ground his head he bow'd
  Piping of his eye.

When the weary day was o'er
  At the hour of five,
Then he watch'd her as before
  Going for a drive.
Every day—a glimpse allow'd,
  She drove happy by,
To the ground his head he bow'd
  Piping of his eye.

Days and months had gone, and still
  Watch'd he on his post,
Till one evening taken ill
  He gave up the ghost.
Morning found the body there
  Lying on its side,
And a Jury did declare
  'Twas a madman died.

HELEN MACKAY'S LAST APPEAL.

In December 1851, John Mackay, widower, and Elizabeth Mackay, his sister, were tried a nd found guilty in the Supreme Court at Calcutta for beating to death Helen, a little girl a few years old, a child of John Mackay by his deceased wife. The story was one of the most horrible in the annals of crime. Speaking of the poor child's body after death, the witnesses all testified that "it was one raw sore." Both the Mackays were sentenced to transportation for life.

Mercy, mercy, spare the lash, oh, strike me not again,
There's a fear upon my heart, aunt, which is keener than
　　the pain ;
A shadow steals before my eyes, a weight subdues my
　　breath,
A faintness is come over me ; oh, aunt, can this be
　　death ?

Is this the death for which I've pray'd from eve till
　　morning's light,
As bruised and bleeding I have lain, through many a
　　weary night,
A death which had no fear for me but ever in my breast
Was heralded by thoughts of hope and dreams of future
　　rest ?

Which told me of that happy land where all earth's
    pangs are o'er,
And where the woes which press me here will trouble
    me no more,
Where little children are beloved, where pains and sor-
    rows cease,
Where the wicked cease from troubling and the weary
    are at peace.

See, cruel aunt, my mother smiles and beckons me
    above,
And calls me from this world of woe to God's eternal
    love ;
Then spare me, spare me future pangs, as you would be
    forgiven,
Send me not bleeding from your lash to testify in
    Heaven.

I've borne full long my painful lot, 'tis over, and
    I go,
I sink beneath the agony of want, and taunt, and blow,
My spirit crush'd, my body gash'd and beaten to the
    tomb,
As life has had no light for me, so death presents no
    gloom.

One other word and I have done; I know my time is
    near,
The hand of death is on me, the hand that seems so
    dear,
But ere my worn-out spirit flies to everlasting rest,
Oh, let my little sister lay her head upon my breast!

And by the sufferings I have known, the agonies I've
    borne,
The broken heart, the hunger, thirst, the flesh so bruised
    and torn,
Oh spare my little sister, oh let my darling live,
And freely as I pardon you, may God your sins forgive.

'Tis over, sister, closer, press me closer to your heart,
Weep not, for it is mercy that now forces us apart,
Now kiss me, Mary darling, another, now good bye,
God calls me to our mother in her home beyond the sky.

TRANSLATION.

LE CHEMIN DU PARADIS.

At a hospice' gate outside,
    A child to see her mother press'd,
" Go," the cruel porter cried,
    " And cease your vain request."
" She's there and her I fain would see,"
        The child replied, and knock'd once more,
        When one of those she did implore,
Said, seeing her tears flow piteously,
      " Poor orphan child
      " Be reconciled,
" Thy mother from this world of vice
" Has ta'en the road to Paradise."

She enquires of them the way,
    Kindly answers every one,
Long the journey is they say,
    Many perils to be run.

Hope, however, leads her ever
    To her pious journey's end,
    Faith doth courage to her lend,
Charity forsakes her never,
    Soon will she
    Her mother see,
For she now believes she flies
On the road to Paradise.

Famish'd, faint, her strength forsakes her
    One night in a desert drear,
By the hand a shepherd takes her,
    Leads her to a convent near;
To her help each sister flies,
    All too late her strength is blighted,
    Death, which parted, reunited
Child and mother in the skies,
    God call'd her to
    Her mother true,
And that poor child no longer sighs
For her home in Paradise.

REPLY TO "FARE THEE WELL AND IF FOR EVER."

Fare thee well and if for ever,
   Then for ever let it be ;
For again, false Byron, never
   Canst thou be beloved by me.

If thy breast were bared before me,
   What a cruel heart 'twould shew ;
False to her who did adore thee—
   Cold as Russia's wastes of snow.

'Twas not I who rent asunder
   Ties which should have lived till death,
Thou hast been a wide world's wonder
   For thy scorn of love and faith.

Vain are now thy magic verses,
   None to pity can they move ;
Better far to send me curses
   Than the mockery of love.

Though the world to soothe endeavour,
    Though it sorrow for my pain,
Can it Byron, can it ever
    Make thy false heart true again?

No, a heart once dead to feeling
    True again can never prove,
And the wound that knows no healing
    Is a woman's trampled love.

Oh! to banish recollection
    Of that early love of mine,
When my young heart's deep affection
    Thought it met the same in thine.

When in tones of gentle kindness
    That false tongue love's accents pour'd ;
Could I think my love was blindness?
    Could I doubt I was adored?

Still there is a tie that binds me
    To respect thy once loved name,
Though each passing morrow finds thee
    Deeper still in guilt and shame.

Yes—our little infant smiling
   As she climbs upon my knee,
Lisping, with her voice beguiling,
   Teaches me to think of thee.

When, as twilight's shadows gather,
   She repeats her ev'ning prayer,
Then she prays for thee, her father,
   Tho' she sees no father there.

Thus it is, though love has vanished
   From this torn and bleeding heart,
That the feeling is not banished
   That thou still my husband art.

Fare thee well, and, if for ever
   In this world of grief and pain,
I will hope that those who sever
   Here will meet elsewhere again.

ACROSTIC.

To a young lady after the death of the gentleman she was engaged to.

Happy may your future be
  After all your sorrow,
Recollect, no woes can e'er
  Rob us of a morrow.
In the future bury then
  Every grief that's past,
Time will aid the careworn heart
  To be glad at last.

Heaven its aid will also send
  Unto all bereaved,
Never yet was any one
  Trusting there deceived:
Every one may gather there
  Resignation in despair.

THE UNION BANK SHAREHOLDER AND THE ROOK.

APRÈS POE.

. Applicable to many poor Shareholders now.

Once upon a midnight dreary as I ponder'd very leery
Over piles of old accounts and with sweat in every
pore—
For the heat it was quite shocking,—I heard a sudden
knocking,
As if somebody was mocking me outside my cham-
ber door.
"'Tis some larky friend," I mutter'd, "mocking me out-
side my door—
"Only this and nothing more."

Ah, distinctly I remember, 'twas in blazing hot Sep-
tember,
And from every streaming member ran the sweat upon
the floor,
For I fear'd I'd have to borrow some tin upon the mor-
row,
And debtors to their sorrow find borrowing a bore,
And most men will acknowledge that 'tis an awful bore
To borrow ever more.

And my throbbing heart's suggestions invented many
    questions
As to who at such a time could be knocking at my door,
And I thought some friend, retreating from some late
    convivial meeting,
 Had come, with curious greeting, a Manilla to implore—
For many are the friends that come Manillas to implore
              From my much respected store.

So I got up, softly creeping, and through the doorway
    peeping
I saw nothing there but darkness around me and before ;
And the silence was unbroken, and not a word or token
Shew'd me that a friend had come a Manilla to im-
    plore :
And no friend having come a Manilla to implore,
             I wonder'd all the more.

I came back very curious, at the same time very
    furious,
When again I heard the knocking somewhat louder
    than before ;
Then said I with much ill-will, " That knocking's at the
    jill-mill,
" And if possible I still will the mystery explore—
" I'll open out the jill-mill and this mystery explore,
          " After that I'll try no more."

Open then the jill-mill throwing, I was not long in
    knowing
What it was that had been knocking as I thought out-
    side my door,
And I fear I somewhat shook as a big and jet-black
    rook,
With a cheeky mien and look, hopp'd and settled on
    the floor,
Then flew and perch'd himself on a bust above my door—
                On a bust of Thomas Moore.

Then he look'd down, as if smiling, on the vouchers I'd
    been filing,
And, my temper sadly riling, croak'd as if his throat
    was sore;
Then my frame with anger shook, and I hurl'd at him
    a book,
But I miss'd that horrid rook sitting there above my
    door;
And I ask'd him for his name, and why he stuck out-
    side my door,
             And the rook croak'd, " Nothing more."

Then I stared almost insanely to hear that rook
    ungainly
Address me in plain English from that bust of Thomas
    Moore;

And on the fact I ponder'd, and frequently I wonder'd,
If my hearing had not blunder'd in those two words
    " Nothing more"—
For I never heard that any bird could croak so plain
    before
                    As that rook did " Nothing more."

And there he sat so knowing, with his eyes so bright
    and glowing,
Looking sideways down at me as I gazed upon the floor,
That I thought not of retiring, but his knowing look
    admiring,
Of myself I kept enquiring if the devil ever bore,
When he came upon the earth to be a horrid bore,
                    A black rook's shape before.

Thus I stood engaged in guessing, till 'twas time to be
    undressing,
And my eyes from staring at the bird were getting
    very sore,
When a bright thought on me shining in the midst of
    my divining,
And all my wits combining, I eyed the black brute o'er,
And I ask'd him when he meant to leave the bust
    above my door,
                    And he croak'd, " Oh, never more."

Then I put another query and I bow'd polite and leery
To that black rook sitting there on the bust of Thomas
    Moore—
"Now, no offence is meant thee, but has the devil sent
    thee?
"Has he like a prophet sent thee to tell me what's in
    store,
"To tell me of my future, if for me there's luck in
    store?"
                Croak'd he, "That and nothing more."

"Prophet," said I, "then be civil if you are a real
    devil,
"I'd like to have an answer to a question or two more ;
"There is scrip upon my table, you may see by many
    a label,
"Of that Joint Stock Bank unstable built by Larpent
    and Tagore :
"But I'll say nothing bad against poor Dwarkanauth
    Tagore—
                "He is gone for evermore.

"Prophet," said I, "bird, or devil, I've been treated very
    evil,
"I've invested in that Bank's shares a very heavy score,

"But I never thought when buying how soon I should
be sighing
"For my tin that then was flying; tell me truly, I implore—
"Tell me shall I get my tin back—tell me truly, I implore."
                              And he croak'd, "Never more."

Then I answer'd, "Oh! the devil, you only seem to revel
" In croaking all that's bad from that bust above my door,
" But please me still by staying, and still more so by say-
ing
"That shareholders who've been paying need not pay any
more."
But that rook with eyes so knowing, and twinkling more
and more,
                              Croak'd loudly, "Plenty more."

Then I cried, with anger smarting, "You'd better be de-
parting,
"For I will not have you croaking your falsehoods o'er
and o'er;
"Leave not a single token of the words that you have
spoken
"Of the great Bank that was broken when it owed at
least a crore;

" Take your shadow from my floor, and leave that bust
   above my door."
                 And he croak'd, " No, never more."

And still he sits so knowing, and has never thought of
   going
From the bust that he thus perch'd upon above my
   chamber door,
And his eyes are always seeming to be with pleasure beaming,
As I often sit here dreaming of my tin in days of yore,
Ere other rooks had gull'd me in the dodging days of
   yore,
                 As I'll be gulled—oh ! never more.

NON CONFUNDAR IN ÆTERNUM.

The prayer of the Czar Nicholas after the Massacre of Sinope.

Let all nations band together,
    Let Great Britain lead the fight,
Let them all their forces gather,
    I will shew them might is right.
With my millions, serf and slave, I
    To their vessels back will turn 'em,
In te, Domine, speravi—
    Non confundar in æternum!

Hark! the war-dogs howling round me—
    Briton, Austrian, Frank, and Turk—
They'll regret that e'er they found me
    Cause to do more dirty work.
If they still my power will brave, I
    With my red-hot shot will burn 'em,
In te, Domine, speravi—
    Non confundar in æternum!

Have I ever proved a liar?
   Landmarks did I ever break?
Did I ever once conspire
   Turkish provinces to take?
No—then let them roar and rave, I
   Place my trust in Thee and spurn 'em,
In te, Domine, speravi—
   Non confundar in æternum!

Did I put my troops in motion
   Where my troops ought not to go,
Till their fleets had scour'd my ocean
   In defence of Russia's foe?
Let all Russia find a grave, I
   Still will fight and still will spurn 'em,
In te, Domine, speravi—
   Non confundar in æternum.

Do not all my Christians know me
   As their great and glorious lord?
Out of all my millions shew me
   One by whom I'm not *adored?*
Six foot three in height and brave, I
   Laugh all foes to scorn and spurn 'em,
In te, Domine, speravi—
   Non confundar in æternum.

Can my conscience e'er reprove me?
     Am not I the Russian Czar?
Should not hordes of those who love me
     Die for me in useless war?
Of them all obedience crave I,
     Even in things that don't concern 'em;
In te, Domine, speravi—
     Non confundar in æternum.

Now let Sinope be witness
     Of the power of shot and shell,
Let that slaughter prove my fitness
     For the hottest place in Hell.
Despot, tyrant, bully, knave, I
     In thy name spit at and spurn 'em,
In te, Domine, speravi—
     Non confundar in æternum.

             1854.

THE A. D. C.

BEST MAN AND CHIEF-MOURNER.

" Last season the female European attendant of a certain noble lady, but just out from England, became the wife of a confidential clerk in a Government Office here ; she was much respected by her mistress, who was herself in the Church the day she was married, and generously presented her with handsome presents ; at the request of her mistress, she was honored by being given away by the principal A. D. C. This year an equal degree of kindly feeling had been manifested towards the lady's maid ; in less than ten months she became a bride, a mother, and a corpse. The A. D. C. again attended to do honor, but this time it was at the funeral."—*Englishman's letter from Simla, 8th July.*

Après Hemans.

In the snowy Himalayas
   Voices were heard in prayer,
'Twas a happy marriage rite,
And every eye was bright,
   And an A. D. C. was there !

For a " noble Lady's" maid,
   Far from her native land,
To a " confidential clerk"
   Was giving heart and hand.

And the 'noble lady' vow'd
  That the rite should honor'd be
By the presence of herself
  And a lordly A. D. C.!!

In the snowy Himalayas
  Voices were raised in prayer,
And 'twas a glorious sight,
That happy marriage rite,
  For an A. D. C. was there!!

But a year had not pass'd o'er
  The head of that young bride,
Ere she became a mother,
  Then sicken'd, pined, and died.

The 'noble lady' grieved for
  Her sad untimely end,
And to the lowly burial
  Her A. D. C. did send!!

In the snowy Himalayas
  Voices were heard in prayer,
'Twas a solemn funeral rite,
But a most imposing sight,
  For an A. D. C. was there!!

Then let her calmly rest
  Where the snow-clad pine-trees wave,
For a lordly A. D. C.
  Attended at her grave!

When A. D. Cs. thus follow
  The lowly to their rest,
Oh! 'twould be wickedness to doubt
  The burial must be bless'd.

Then, husband, do not mourn her,
  That young and loving wife,
For surely she was honor'd
  In death as when in life.

In the snowy Himalayas
  Voices were heard in prayer,
'Twas a solemn funeral rite,
But a most imposing sight,
  For an A. D. C. was there!!

THE BENGALEE " BOY JONES."

Or the story of the Coolie who would see Lord Dalhousie asleep in bed.

Ladies—come and read the story
    Of the coolie, brave and bold,
Who for neither gain nor glory
    Storm'd the great Dalhousie's hold ;
Not for murder did he do it—
    Robbery his soul abhorr'd—
His intention—would you know it—
    Was to see a sleeping lord !

Surely 'twas a curious notion
    For the man to entertain !
In a state of sad commotion
    Must have been the coolie's brain.
Were the lord a pretty lady,
    Men might fairly risk the chance
Of a fine from wrathful Cadi*
    For one single happy glance.

* Wrathful Cadi, *i. e.*, Sir Solomon Slily, or Macleod Wyllie.

Half the hours of night were number'd,
  Shone the bright moon over head,
Nearly everybody slumber'd—
  All at least who were in bed,
When the coolie, nothing daunted
  By the armèd watch and ward,
Roused his soul, Dalhousie-haunted,
  For a visit to the lord.

Not a single lamp was burning
  In Dalhousie's lofty halls,
But the moon at every turning
  Brightly shone upon the walls ;
Shone in every nook and corner,
  Shone in every hall and room,
Shone out like a brilliant scorner
  Of such things as night or gloom.

And throughout that lordly dwelling
  Not a sound the silence stirr'd,
Save when some wild jackall's yelling
  From the neighbouring plain was heard ;
Or when clank of spur or sabre
  Of the sentries on the stair,
Or the snore of heavy sleeper
  Broke upon the midnight air.

And the moon shone out more brightly,
  And the silence reign'd more deep,
As our hero, treading lightly,
  Went to see the lord asleep !
Past the bayonet, past the sabre,
  Past the guards, our hero went,
No suspicions did they harbour
  Of the coolie's odd intent.

Thus he spake to every sentry,
  Thus to all the guard he said,
" Pray excuse my ill-timed entry
  " When I ought to be in bed ;
" But this evening, dreadful error,
  " In the Dome my tools I left,
" And I'm in the greatest terror,
  " Almost of my mind bereft.

" Much I fear my vengeful master
  " Will enforce his rigid rules,
" Cutting, oh, the dread disaster,
  " My month's tullub for the tools ! !
" Let me therefore, sentry, go there,
  " Let me therefore go upstairs,
" For I really think I know where
  " I did leave them unawares."

Thus he spake to every sentry,
　　As the tears roll'd down his cheek,
Thus he gain'd an easy entry
　　To the room that he did seek ;
There, before the chamber sprawling,
　　Slept the watchful Jemadar—
O'er that sleeper gently crawling,
　　Nothing now his way can bar !

See, upon a bed reposing,
　　With his head upon his arm,
See the great Dalhousie dozing
　　In a slumber soft and calm !
There he lay, that awful being,
　　Idol of the coolie's soul !
Who can guess what soft delirium
　　O'er that coolie's senses stole ?

As he stood, in wonder staring
　　At the great recumbent lord,
Hardly breathing, never daring
　　To ejaculate a word ;
With wide-open eyes admiring,
　　Wondering such a sight to see,
Of his little self enquiring
　　What the sleeper's dreams might be.

1

Was he dreaming of the millions
  Which his tullub made *in pice,*
Of his horses and postillions,
  Of his dholl, his ghee, his rice?
Was he dreaming of the pleasure
  He should have in after days,
When upon his lakhs of treasure
  Gloating eyes would fondly gaze?

Thus the coolie stood in wonder
  Till he thought it time to go,
Then he made his awful blunder—
  Fool! how could he blunder so?
Not content with the uncertain
  Light upon the lord asleep,
He must open out the curtain
  For a nearer, clearer peep.

Slowly pull'd he out the curtain,
  Gently squeezed himself inside,
And again, for one short moment,
  With delight the sleeper eyed;
But, alas! in that same moment
  Something on the silence broke,
And his lordship on a sudden
  With a gentle start awoke.

Oh! the horror of the coolie,
    And the noble lord's surprise,
When the latter, coming slowly
    To his senses, fix'd his eyes
On his wretched victim, staring,
    Trembling now in every limb,
With Dalhousie's fierce eyes glaring
    Like a tiger's full at him!

" Who the devil are you, fellow?
    " What the devil do you here?"
Loudly did his lordship bellow
    At the poor man, white from fear.
" Here, chuprassee, jemadar,
    " Here you sleeping lazy soors,"—
At his cries from near and far
    In they rush'd through all the doors.

Jemadar and kidmutgar,
    Peon, chupprassee, bearers all,
Havildar and duffadar,
    Aides-de-Camp both short and tall,
On the poor devoted coolie
    Most courageously they rush'd,
And with treatment most unruly
    Here and there their victim push'd;

Till at last with one tremendous
    Burst the coolie took his flight,
From such jumps may Heaven defend us,
    As he took on that same night ! !
Down the staircase wildly rushing,
    Jumping twenty steps outright,
Past the sentries fiercely pushing,
    Who can stop his frantic flight?

Vain the speed of every bearer,
    Vain the Aides-de-Camps' fierce chase,
Not a single man got nearer,
    None could go the coolie's pace ;—
Past the bayonet, past the sabre,
    Past the guard, the gate, the wall,
Till he got to Diamond Harbour
    Never stopp'd that man at all.

THE SONG OF DEATH,

CAWNPORE.

———

With body wasted and worn,
  With a heart as heavy as lead,
A woman sat where her husband's form
  On the blood-stain'd floor lay dead!
Women and children, wild
  With hunger, round her press'd;
One little babe, her infant child,
  Was starving on her breast,
And thus with weary song she lull'd
  Her dying child to rest;—

" Roar—roar—roar !—
  Oh! that dread incessant din
From the enemy's guns without,
  And our own few guns within!
Shell, and musket, and gun,
  Gun, and musket, and shell,
Mingle their roar with our groans and shrieks,
  And turn this place into Hell!

" Roar—roar—roar !—
    Will those hideous guns ne'er cease?
Roar !—roar—roar—
    Must death be our sole release?
Must all, the good, the brave,
    The young and the old, thus die?
Must we vainly pray to Him to save?
    To God must we vainly cry?

" Death—Death—Death !
    In every shape and form,
Death, Death, Death,
    Rides on the iron storm !
He comes with the hurtling shot,
    He comes with the bursting shell,
While wounds, starvation, and disease
    Do his dread work too well.

" I have lost my husband dear,
    Two brothers and their wives,
And while my life is wearing out
    Death takes my children's lives !
Oh !—Death—Death—Death !
    'Mid misery, hunger, and woe,
My last child dying, my husband dead,
    I court thy friendly blow.

" And why should I shrink from Death
    When my dear ones all are gone?
Their lives were ended in want and woe,
    And why not thus my own?
Oh! husband, good and kind,
    Oh! ever dear to me,
Oh! why should thy wife remain behind
    When Death has taken thee?

" Death—Death—Death!—
    I hear the weary mean
Of another sobbing wife reply
    To her husband's dying groan?
And I hear the dreadful oaths
    Of a soldier in his pain;
Another hour that wretched man
    Will never curse again.

" Death—Death—Death!—
    'Neath yon embankment there,
A husband tends his wounded wife,
    And friends kneel round in prayer!
Their tears fall thick and fast
    On that blood-stain'd, blood-red, sod,
As their dying friend's last torture past,
    Her soul takes flight to God!

" Death—Death—Death !—
   You fever'd woman seems
To be happy 'mid those joyous scenes
   Which come but in her dreams;
But her weary wasted form,
   Her fiercely burning head,
Proclaim that soon her troubles o'er
   She, too, must join the dead.

" Last week her husband fell
   Shot down close by her side,
And then her grey-hair'd mother
   In that burning barrack died !
Her only sister follow'd
   Struck by a bursting shell,
To-morrow she will join them all
   Down in that hideous well.*

" Oh ! were my loved ones all
   Once more in life again,
Oh ! were they only safe from here,
   From all this grief and pain ;

---

* Every evening a burial party was told-off to throw into the well the bodies of all who had been killed, or had died during the previous day.

From all this carnage, woe, and strife
   To see them safely fly,
How gladly would I yield my life,
   How gladly would I die !"

With body wasted and worn,
   With a heart as heavy as lead,
A woman nursed her dying child,
   Her husband, near her, dead.
   Death—Death—Death
In weary tones, with gasping breath,
   'Mid misery, sickness, wounds, and woe,
'Mid the cannon's roar and the yells of the foe,
   She sang this song about Death—

Her husband's corpse was thrown
   That evening in the well,
Whose black deep mouth for victims yawn'd
   Like one of the mouths of Hell.
   Death—Death—Death—
Her babe, her last, was dead,
   Heart-broken, from that bloody floor
   She rose and stagger'd to the door,
   Then pass'd out to return no more ;
The stars shone overhead ;

The cannon's roar, the foes' wild yell
(Her child's, her own, her husband's, knell)
   Upon her ear unheeded fell,
As, pressing to her broken heart
The babe from which she could not part,
   She plunged into the well.

THE WIFE'S WELCOME.

They lived apart for four years, waiting for the decree divorcing
her from her first husband, and then they were married.

Four long years ago we parted,
　Four long years ago,
Silent, sobbing, broken-hearted,
From my burning eyelids started
　Tears of real woe ;
All my soul within me sinking,
　How I clung to thee!
From all words of comfort shrinking,
Only of our parting thinking,
　Dead I wish'd to be !

Four long years of silent sorrow,
　Four long weary years,
Every day renew'd to-morrow
With no solace whence to borrow
　Comfort in my fears ;
By no smile of kind friend gladden'd,
　Still I waited on,
By my blighted hopes near madden'd,
Sickness-stricken, spirit-sadden'd,
　Till four years were gone.

Then at last the silver lining
  Of my clouded life
Shone from Heaven and now is shining
  On a happy wife ;
And she cries with heart-felt feeling
  As she clings to thee,
From her eyes the bright drops stealing,
All her pent-up love revealing,
  " Welcome back to me,
" Welcome, dear long absent husband,
" Welcome to the heart that mourn'd thee,
" Welcome to the eyes that wept thee,
" Welcome back to me."

HOME SICKNESS.

Suggested by verses under that name, in "Household Words,"
about ten years ago.

WHERE we are, our hearts are wandering
 Far across the white sea-foam,
Christmas still renews the longing
 For our dear old Island Home,
Every English heart in India
 Pines its native land to see,
Evermore we long to settle
 Where we fain would be.

Where we are—'mid gorgeous flowers—
 Rose and dahlia blossom fair,
And the pale-white, day-closed cereus
 Opens to the evening air.
Daisy, buttercup, and lily,
 Lilac, and laburnum-tree,
Deck the meadow and the garden,
 Where we fain would be.

Where we are, the Bulbul only
    Warbles forth his scarce-heard lay,
Birds of every hue and plumage
    Through the jungles wing their way.
Linnet, robin, thrush, and cuckoo
    Pour their notes from hedge and tree,
And the skylark wakes the morning,
    Where we fain would be.

Where we are, broad plains and jungle
    Make at best a dreary view,
Unrelieved by oak or beech-tree,
    Or the graceful bending yew.
Hill and valley, woodland, meadow,
    And the ever glorious sea,
Are where we in childhood wander'd,
    Where we fain would be.

Where we are, the stately Banian
    Stretches far across the glade,
But beneath it cobras nestle
    And the tiger finds a shade.
Under oak and elm our children
    Ramble, from all danger free,
By that lake or rippling streamlet,
    Where we fain would be.

Where we are, a thousand fire-flies
   Sparkle in the autumn night,
And the myriad stars of Heaven
   Elsewhere never shine so bright,
But the star-showers in the moonlight
   Flash along the deep blue sea,
And the golden glowworm glistens,
   Where we fain would be.

Here no sound of scythe or sickle,
   Here no reaper's song is heard,
With the tinkling of the sheep-bell
   Here the air is never stirred.
Strains of feather'd warblers mingle
   With the reaper's song of glee,
With the pleasant low of cattle,
   Where we fain would be.

Where we are, the Sabbath service
   Calls us with such measured peal,
Slow and mournful, that upon us
   English Sabbath memories steal.
How we miss that tuneful chiming,
   When we trod the verdant lea,
From each little village belfry,
   Where we fain would be.

Where we are, our thoughts are ever
    Many thousand miles away,
Where the grey-hair'd mother watches
    O'er our little ones at play,
And, in fancy's dream, the rafter
    Echoes to their shouts of glee,
Would that we could share their laughter,
    Where we fain would be.

HIAWATHA IN CALCUTTA.

1859.

CHAPTER THE FIRST.

Sir Mawdun Lawson Swell-well.

Should you ask me whence these verses,
Whence this parody in doggrel,
All about a learned Justice,—
With his bumptious ways and manners,
With his plans for reformation,
And his fondness for a squabble
With the Bar and the Attornies,
And in fact with everybody,
Like some cross-grained village terrier,
Or Columbia's "Snapping Turtle,"—

I should answer, I should tell you,
"From the Bench of the Supreme Court,
When Sir Mawdun Swell-well's sitting
Either singly at the Sessions,

Trying divers rogues and villains,
Bullying witnesses and jury,
Witnesses, police, and jury;
Or when with his brother Jaksun
He sits hearing suits and causes
On the Plea side or in Chancery,
Or some dreary dry demurrer,
Or some sharp contested motion
For Injunction and Receiver;
Sometimes ogling purdah women,
Through the half-closed doors of palkees;
Sometimes on his knee judicial
Dangling little Hindoo infants,
Praying to the Court for guardians,
Quite oblivious of the vermin
Dropping from their sable bodies;
Sometimes bothering a Counsel,
Sometimes badgering a witness,
Sometimes sneering at Attornies,
Snapping right and left around him,
Like Columbia's ' Snapping Turtle;'
Or when, as Commissioner Swell-well,
He refuses his protection
To each penniless Insolvent,
Till all those who come before him,
Fearing lest they be imprison'd,
Only ask for an adjournment.

Or when, as a Judge in Chambers,
Swell-well takes the Chamber business,
Quarrelling with the meek Attornies,
And the often meeker Counsel :
Commenting upon the practice
And proceedings in this country."

If still further you should ask me,
Saying " Who is this Mawdun ?
Tell us of the Judge Sir Mawdun,
Of Sir Mawdun Lawson Swell-well"—

I should answer, I should tell you,
Straightway in such words as follow :
" Near the Halls of Old Westminster,
In its dusty legal purlieus,
Studied once a would-be member
Of the learned Bar of England.
Not much time he spent in reading,
Little time he spent in mugging—
Skill'd was he in sports and pastimes,
In the merry dance, the Polka ;
In the play of quoits and rackets ;—
Very skilful too at cricket,
Batting, bowling, long-stop, fielding,
None could stand before his bowling ;

Rarely could they take his wicket,
Save when he had taken luncheon ;—
Skill'd was he in playing billiards,
Cues and balls, the game of billiards,
Making, with the right or left hand,
With the cue, or butt, or jigger,
Wondrous hazards, screws, and cannons ;
So skill'd that he might have made at
Pyramids and Pool a living.
Skill'd he also was in shooting,
Never missing snipe or partridge,
With his gun, his ' Westly Richards,'
Double-barrell'd ' Westly Richards.'
Quick and clever too at sparring,
Clever was he with his mawleys.
Young Dutch Sam, Crib, Hannan, Randall,
Scarce were better with their mawleys,
Cabmen, Navvies, Beaks, and Blackguards
All went down before his mawleys !
And he long was called the Chicken,
Styled ' the plucky West-end Chicken,'
Nurses, servant-girls, and barmaids
Loved the plucky West-end Chicken.
Varying study with such pastimes,
Mr. Swell-well, sucking Lawyer,
Pass'd his terms and eat his muttons.

Then (devour'd his prentice muttons)
Call'd unto the Bar behold him,
Very grave and very learned,
But 'twas long before the public
Knew that he was very learned.
In the Halls of old Westminster,
In its ancient Courts of Justice,
Long upon the hindmost benches,
In his gown of stuff, and briefless,
Sate he all unknown and briefless,
Dreaming of forensic honors,
Dreaming of big briefs and guineas,
Dreaming of the Bench and Woolsack.
Seeing through the dreamy vista
Of a long forensic future,
Briefs and Guineas, Bench and Woolsack,
Till a pitying kind Attorney
(How he loved that kind Attorney!)
On the poor youth took compassion,
Handing him a common motion;
Then a brief of fair dimensions,
With his name endorsed as Junior;
Then, again upon the Circuit,
Now and then a prosecution,
Or defence at the Assizes,
Mark'd him as a ' rising Junior.'

Step by step he climb'd the ladder,
Climb'd the ladder of preferment,
Till at last his star of fortune
Rose, and he became a Sergeant :
Silk-gown'd in the foremost Benches,
Full of common law and logic,
Full of statute law and quibbles,
Full of law in *all* its branches,
Soon he earn'd a reputation
As a Nisi Prius Lawyer,
As a deep-read Chancery Lawyer,
As a Parliamentary Lawyer.
Then no more he play'd at rackets,
No more heard the shouts at cricket,
' Ah, you muff, you butter-fingers !'
No more heard the marker shouting,
' Green on yellow, brown's your player,
' Yellow's dead ; will yellow star, Sir ?'
No more crushing blows deliver'd
On the nose of beak or blackguard ;
No more flirted with the barmaids ;
No more kissed the black-eyed nurses ;
But stuck close to his profession,
And increased his reputation,
And at last a vacant Judgeship,
Object of his long ambition,

Offer'd was for his acceptance.—
Never paused he for a moment,
But accepted of the offer,
Kicking up his heels and skipping,
And became a Judge Colonial—
Puisne Justice at Calcutta,
And at once of course was knighted,
And was ' Sir' instead of Serjeant.
Then he came out to Calcutta,
To this hot and broiling city,
To this land of lying niggers,
To this land of sun and niggers.
Such the history of Mawdun,
Such the story of Sir Mawdun,
Of Sir Mawdun Lawson Swell-well."

Ye who love an hour's amusement
In this dreary dull Calcutta,
In this dull and dreary city,—
Go some morning, when you've leisure,
Go and listen to Sir Mawdun,
When upon the Bench he's sitting,
Go and pass an hour with Swell-well:
Then you'll say, as doth the writer,
That ' an hour with Swell-well's' pleasant,
Pleasant is ' an hour with Swell-well.'

CHAPTER THE SECOND.

Sir Mawdun Swell-well and the Peace-Pipe.

On the morning he was sworn in
On the Bench of the Supreme Court,
When the usual oaths he'd taken,
Puisne Judge, Sir Mawdun Swell-well,
From the Bench of the Supreme Court,
With a smile of grave decorum,
Bowing to the Bar, descended.
Then he walk'd unto his Chambers,
And he called his son unto him,
Call'd his little boy unto him,
Saying, " Oh, my little Swell-well,
Oh, my little sucking Lawyer,
In your father's eyes an Infant,
In the eyes of Law an Infant ;
But my Clerk, although an Infant,
Go and call the tribes of Lawyers,
Go and call them all together,
Tell them 'tis a Judge's summons,
Tell them 'tis a Judge's order,
To attend him at his Chambers.
Run my child, my legal Infant,
Call the tribes of Law together ;
I await them at my Chambers."

Straightway ran the infant Swell-well
Down the staircase without stopping,
From the Chambers to the Court House,
To the room of the Attornies,
To the library of the Counsel,
All along the long verandah,
Up and down each winding staircase,
Into every room and office,
Hopping, skipping, shouting, screaming,
" Come, oh Counsel, come Attornies,
Come unto my Governor's Chambers:
Listen to your Judge's Summons,
And obey your Judge's Order."
Forth they came, the tribes of Lawyers,
Silk-gown'd Counsel, grave Attornies,
Public Notaries and Proctors,
Leaving bags and briefs behind them,
Leaving bills of costs behind them;
Tripping over one another,
Pushing forward without stopping,
Soon they reach'd Sir Mawdun's Chambers,
Stood within Judge Swell-well's Chambers.
Then he spoke to them in this wise,
Stretching over them his right hand,
Smiling with a grave decorum:
" Hearken unto me, ye Lawyers,
Members of the same profession:

I'm your father, you're my children,—
Listen to the words of wisdom
Which upon my lips are hovering.
I have come from old Westminster,
From those Halls of Law and Justice,
From her famous Courts of Justice ;
I have cross'd the big-sea water
To this land of sun and niggers ;
To this land of virtuous niggers ;
I've been made your Puisne Justice,
And I mean to do full justice
To my berth and high position.
I've been told that in this country
White men, speaking of these natives,
In derision call them niggers,
Call them cheating, lying niggers ;
Saying that 'they can't be beaten
At the game of fraud and falsehood.'
I have also heard with sorrow,
When at home, the old tradition
Of the merchant of Calcutta,—
That he is not altogether
' Quite the thing, the clean Potato ;'
That just like his lordly dwelling,
Now and then he needs a white-wash.
I have also heard that tradesmen
Charge the most tremendous prices,

And with tempting words and civil,
And with promises of credit,
Lead the soft unwary youngster
To the dogs and to the devil.
I have heard, too, that you Lawyers,
When you get the chance of plunder,
Take the chance and make the plunder :—
Of the Union Bank the story
Is not even yet forgotten."

Here he paused.   The mighty speaker
Paused to cough and clear his thorax :
Either had a stray musquito
Flown into his throat and stuck there,
Causing pain and irritation ;
Or, the speaker's strong emotion
Choked his utterance for a moment,
For he cough'd to clear his thorax.
Then, his cranium gravely shaking,
Thus the learned Judge proceeded :

" All these things are very wicked,
And, to my mind, very shocking.—
Why should natives be called niggers,
And be treated with derision ?
Why should these Calcutta merchants
Not be rich until they're white-wash'd ?

Why should tradesmen, with huge prices,
Tempting words, and credit system,
Lead the unwary to their ruin?
Why should Lawyers seek for plunder?
Oh my children! Oh my Lawyers!
I have come to stop this scandal,
To improve your ways of business;
In this careless sinful city
I will be a Great Reformer,
And all fraud will sternly punish :—
I will not allow Insolvents
To go scathless from my presence;
And if you will do your duty,
And in all things aid and help me,
You will prosper, I shall prosper,
And the public too will prosper.
Go, my children, tell the public
All that I have said this morning;
But before you leave my presence,
That we may be friends together,
That we all may know each other,
Stay and smoke a friendly peace-pipe :
Let us smoke a pipe together."

Then upon the chairs he made them
Sit down in a crowd before him;

And he order'd out his Pipe-box,
Order'd out his best Tobacco,
Order'd out his large Cigar-case :
And Sir Mawdun Lawson Swell-well
Fill'd a short clay-pipe with Bird's-eye ;
Darkly brown the bowl was color'd
With some years of steady smoking.
And he made his little Infant
Hand around to all the Lawyers
Pipes, Cigars, Cheroots, Tobacco.—
Some preferr'd a Clay or Meerschaum
Fill'd with Cavendish or Dog's-nose,
Negro-head, or Latakia,
Shag, Returns, or Prince's mixture :
Others chose Cheroots, Manillas,
Chose the number 3 Manillas.
Some, to smoking not accustom'd,
Took Cigars, the mild Havannahs ;
While a few, with Indian habits,
Call'd for Gools and smoked the Hookah :—
Only did the native Lawyers
Use the handy Hubble-bubble.
There they sat, the tribes of Lawyers,
In Sir Mawdun Swell-well's Chambers ;
Sat and smoked an hour in silence ;—
Not a sound disturb'd the silence
Save the bubbling Hubble-bubble,

And the spitting of the Lawyers
As they sat and smoked the Peace-Pipe,—
Smoked the Pipe of Peace together.
Then, with one accord, they parted,
Bowing lowly to Sir Mawdun;
Who, with his right hand extended,
Once more in this wise address'd them;
"Oh my children, let this Peace-Pipe
Which we now have smoked together,—
Let our Pipe of Peace remind you
That you are my friends henceforward,
That we'll all be friends together."
And he added, "Now good morning :"
And they answer'd, " Sir, good morning."

"OUR VISITING BRETHREN,"

As sung in Lodge "Excelsior."

" You may roam through the world."

1.

You may roam through this place some new pleasure to
    seek,
  And in search of excitement may try every dodge,
But, wherever you go any day in the week,
    You'll enjoy yourselves most when you visit this
      Lodge.
For if hearts that glow like burning coal,
  Full of social love and right good cheer,
Are comrades who most delight the soul,
    You're sure to enjoy yourselves when you come here.
      Then remember whenever for fun you're in-
      clined,
        When at home disengaged and with no-
        thing to do,
      On the first and third Tuesday of each month
      you'll find
        'Mid the hearts of 'Excelsior' a welcome
        for you.

2.

Our Lodge is a young one, an infant in years,
  Of antiquity's honors it cannot yet boast,
Yet it already feels that true love which endears
  To a visiting Brother the heart of his host.
Yes, we Excelsiors feel that ' mystic tie'
  Which binds alike the rich and poor,
And with kindly heart and beaming eye
  We welcome all who enter our door.
        Then remember whenever for fun you're in-
          clined,
          When at home disengaged and with no-
            thing to do,
        On the first and third Tuesday of each month
          you'll find
          'Mid the hearts of ' Excelsior' a welcome
            for you.

3.

Our guests here to-night will, we hope, come again
  To join in our work and partake of our cheer,
And let them not think that they come here in vain,
  For they help us upstairs and they gladden us here.
For ' Excelsior' loves her guests to see
  Where her songs are sung and her wine is pour'd,
And those guests to please their hosts should be
  A host in themselves at her festive board.

Then remember whenever for fun you're in-
    clined,
    When at home disengaged and with nothing
        to do,
On the first and third Tuesday of each month
    you'll find
    'Mid the hearts of ' Excelsior' a welcome
        for you.

EXCELSIOR!

As sung at Lodge "Excelsior."

The hours of night are waning fast,
The eating part of our repast
Is done, and now, with wine and ice,
We chant this song, and chorus thrice,
EXCELSIOR!

Our Master is a Mason meek,
Who tells you with the greatest cheek
These lines are his,—an artful dodge
To sing the praises of his Lodge
EXCELSIOR!

His brow surrounded with a wreath
Of white smoke curling through his teeth—
He sings not—never has he sung—
But calls for songs with oily tongue,
EXCELSIOR.

He'd make us stay all night if we·
Would but remain—that cannot be;
From loving wife or sister dear
We do not wish this taunt to hear,
        " EXCELSIOR ! ! !"

" Beware," the Wardens say, " beware,
" Beware that Master debonair,
" A man must be, with him to chaff,
" All unconcern'd while others laugh,
        EXCELSIOR."

" Oh stay," Tom Jones implores, " oh stay !
" Upon the bones I have to play,
" Not Davey Carson on the bones
" Can vie with me, Past-Master Jones,
        EXCELSIOR."

Our evening o'er, at home arrived,
We preach the good we have derived,
And pour into our loved one's ear
The merits of the Lodge so dear,
        EXCELSIOR.

And thus the praises that we get
From her on whom our love is set,

" My dear, my pet, how very nice,
" How very free from aught like vice,
          Excelsior!!!"

In after days, when old and grey,
We'll think of evenings pass'd away,
Of fun, songs, glees, and nigger bones
And banjos played by Thomas Jones,
          " Excelsior."

THE ENTERED APPRENTICE'S TOAST.

As sung in Lodge "Excelsior."

Come pass round the bowl, let each jovial soul
  Fill a bumper on this great occasion,
Though not on our legs we must toast to the dregs
  The health of our newly-made Mason.

But first let us teach, in a song, not a speech
  Like a padre who puts a grave face on,
What we always expect, in this sect so select,
  From a Free and an Accepted Mason.

We first insist on, as a sine quâ non,
  That a man has a good reputation,
None can enter our camp, who's a tramp, leg, or scamp,
  A "bad lot" we won't make a Mason.

Then we "secresy" preach, not to tell what we teach,
  And this is his chief obligation,
In all time to come let his watchword be "mum"
  As to all that he knows as a Mason.

His wife with her wiles, with her tears and her smiles,
   While she gets him her dresses to lace on,
Her sweet lips will pout, and will try to find out
   All her darling has learnt as a Mason.

He's not married, perhaps, and like other soft chaps
   Has some girl his affections to place on,
She will wheedle and kiss, and in moments of bliss
   Try to coax from him what is a Mason.

Bricks and mortar he'll spurn, while he'll masonry learn,
   Cementing that friendly relation,
Which we all understand as the hip, heart, and hand
   Of a Free and an Accepted Mason.

Not a stone, brick, or clod, not a trowel or hod,
   In the boards which our secrets we trace on,
Yet he'll find that we fix the full value on bricks,
   For a " Brick" is each worthy Freemason.

And soon he will know how our hearts overflow,
   Whate'er be our rank or our station,
With charity true, ever ready to do
   All we can for a poor brother Mason.

One other word yet, he must never forget
    To come here on every occasion,
And this we expect, for he must recollect
    We, Excelsiors, have made him a Mason.

Now let's make the most of this excellent toast,
    And for preaching make some reparation,
For though the world owns there are sermons in stones,
    Preaching is not the forte of a Mason,—
Here's the health of our newly-made Mason.

THE TYLER'S TOAST.

As sung in Lodge " Excelsior."

Hard times, come again no more.

Let us pause in our banquet and cease a while our cheer,
    While we all drink kindly to the poor,
'Tis a toast that should ever find hearty welcome here,
    Oh, hard times, come again no more.
To the poor, the sad, and the weary,
    Hard times, hard times, come again no more,
Far too long you have linger'd with those who suffer sore,
    Oh, hard times, come again no more.

While we laugh through our revel and all around are
        gay,
    There are strong men starving on the moor,
There are poor fainting children who for a morsel pray,
    While hard hearts drive them from the door.
To the poor, the sad, and the weary,
    Hard times, hard times, come again no more,
Far too long you have linger'd with those who suffer sore,
    Oh, hard times, come again no more.

There are shrieks from the shipwreck'd across the stormy
    wave,
Wild groans 'mid the battle's fearful roar,
There are deep moans of sorrow from mourners round a
    grave,
    Aye, sad hearts at sea and on shore.
To the poor, the sad, and the weary,
    Hard times, hard times, come again no more,
Far too long you have linger'd with those who suffer
    sore,
    Oh, hard times, come again no more.

There's the sigh of the guilty, of the lost, of the betray'd,
    Sad prayers which from Heaven aid implore,
Wail of widow'd wife and husband, of lover, and of maid,
    For hearts that beat again no more.
To the poor, the sad, and the weary,
    Hard times, hard times, come again no more,
Far too long you have linger'd with those who suffer
    sore,
    Oh, hard times, come again no more.

IN MEMORIAM.

'Twas with plunging, trembling motion upon a troubled
    ocean,
Through the raging, swelling waters that our vessel
    forced her way,
And a day of grief was dawning as the night gave way
    to morning,
When in her dismal cabin my young wife dying lay.

All that night she had been raving with a sad and
    piteous craving
For the mother whom she doted on with more than
    woman's love,
And her sunken brown eyes glisten'd with madness
    when she listen'd
To the waters raging round her and the wind that howl'd
    above.

When quiet she seem'd sitting while the twilight hours
    were flitting
In the little home in Jersey with her mother by her side,
And her children nestled round her and with chains
    of sea-weed bound her,
As with all of them she prattled in the pleasant evening
    tide.

And thoughts of heavenly glories mingled with the
childhood's stories
She had taught her little darlings in their Channel
Island Home,
When they stroll'd the beach together in the balmy
summer weather,
And cull'd the sea's bright treasures amid the rocks and
foam.

Again all broken-hearted she wept for the departed,
For the brother who had left them in the spring time
of his life,
And across each sad reflection came some other recollection
From the thousand wandering fancies with which her
brain was rife.

Ah, mercy, how she wander'd while with bleeding
heart I ponder'd
On her pure and stainless life that so speedily must
end,
On the faith that never fail'd her, on the love that ever
hail'd her
Perfect daughter, sister, mother, perfect wife, and perfect friend.

Her thoughts at last grew clearer and she drew me
    nearer, nearer,
To that scarcely beating heart which was ever true to
    me,
And her weary face seem'd lighter and her sunken eyes
    shone brighter
As she gazed upon the husband she never more might
    see.

Ah, the bursting sobs that choked me when my dying
    wife invoked me,
To forgive her all her failings and think of her at her
    best,
And tenderly caressing her husband, with a blessing
On the dear ones she was leaving, she pass'd unto her
    rest.

Deep, deep, beneath the billow, the restless sea her pillow,
(Beneath no weeping willow, beneath no flower-strewn
    sod),
She sleeps, while hearts are breaking, the sleep that
    knows no waking,
Till the Angels come from Heaven and take her to her
    God.

                          July, 1861.

AH, BROKEN IS THE GOLDEN BOWL.

" Or ever the silver cord be loosed, or the golden bowl be broken."

Ah, broken is the golden bowl,
    And loosed the silver cord,
And waiting is her gentle soul
    The summons of her Lord.

The wave, which should have borne her Home
    Upon its surging crest,
Now plunges on 'mid spray and foam
    Above her place of rest.

The breeze, which should have helped that life
    We pray'd to Heaven to save,
Now murmurs 'mid the wild waves' strife
    A requiem o'er her grave.

That mother, praying all in vain
    That God will soon restore
Her darling to herself again,
    Will see her child no more.

The locks of age which yesterday
    Upon her care-worn brow
Were only sprinkled o'er with grey
    Are white with sorrow now.

And tiny hands are clasp'd in hers,
    While childhood's wailing cry
In that sad Home the silence stirs,
    " Why did their mother die ?"

The husband in whose arms she died
    Must bend unto the blow,
Must cross again the restless tide
    Where all he loved lies low.

Then try to bear his heavy load
    And, like his buried wife,
Keep only on that narrow road
    She ever trod through life.

That when again the golden bowl
    Is broken, and the cord
Of silver loosed, his weary soul
May hear with her at Heaven's goal
    The summons of their Lord.

THERESA YELVERTON.

On the news of her defeat in the House of Lords being communicated to her.

Sorrow-stricken, broken-hearted, to the ground fell poor
    Theresa,
Death with all his icy coldness in that moment seem'd
    to seize her;
Not a shriek, or groan, or murmur, did she utter as a
    token
That her hopes were crush'd for ever, that her loving
    heart was broken.
They could only see her anguish, as with gentle hands
    they raised her,
And with words of kindly comfort for her long endur-
    ance praised her,
Bid her hope and still remember in her hour of bitter
    sorrow
That the night is ever darkest when 'tis nearest to the
    morrow;
Told her how behind the tempest always bright the
    sun is shining,
That each gloomy cloud above us ever has its silver
    lining;

Pray'd her not to be discouraged, spoke of all the ties
that bound her,
Of the help she still would meet with from the many
friends around her;
Show'd her how she yet might conquer, that her cause
was well defended,
That in spite of this defeat her noble struggle was
not ended.
Thus they soothed her broken spirit, raised once more
a better feeling,
Till they saw that through her bosom gentle Hope
again was stealing;
Then they left her to her sorrow, on her knees before
her Maker,
And she pray'd with Christian meekness that her God
would not forsake her;

Pray'd for courage in her trials, that her hopes might
not be blighted,
That her cause some day might triumph, and her cruel
wrongs be righted;
Pray'd for him who thus to misery her loving heart had
driven;
Pray'd, whatever else should happen, that he might be
forgiven.

THE DESERTED DISTRICT.

The moan of the district in want of the fair sex.

Ride the planters up and down,
Each one muttering with a frown,
" Not a petticoat or gown,
    Woe is me, tea-planter."

Here and there policeman strays,
Groaning o'er the public ways,
" Not a crinoline or stays,
    " Woe is me, Policeman."

Grumbles each assistant flat,
As he mourns o'er this and that,
" Not a single pork-pie hat,
    " Woe is me, assistant."

And each poor shopkeeping wight
Takes his walk in piteous plight,
" Not a single girl in sight,
    " Woe is me, shopkeeper."

And the poor civilian too
Sighs " Ah, me, what shall I do ?
" Not a single billet-doux,
   Woe is me, civilian."

And the regimental swell,
As he mourns each absent belle,
Votes the place an awful sell,
   " Woe is me, poor soldier."

Not one saucer bonnet there,
Not one face at which to stare,
Not a laugh or sigh to share,
Not a single lock of hair,
   Woe is o'er that district !

TO LITTLE L——Y.

On her first birthday with a present of a Prayer-book and Bible.

" Suffer little children and forbid them not to come unto me, for of such is the Kingdom of Heaven."

Crowds are gather'd round a Teacher
　　On Judæa's favour'd shore,
Humbly list'ning to the Preacher,
　　Raptured with his holy lore ;
Prince and peasant, youth and maiden,
　　Poor and wealthy, priest and sage,
Sickness-stricken, sorrow-laden,
　　Happy youth and hoary age,
Traveller with his heavy burden,
　　Fisherman from Galilee,
Pressing o'er the swelling Jordan,
　　How they flock their Lord to see !

While his words entrance each hearer,
　　While those blessed accents flow,
Mothers press their children nearer
　　Bidding them to Jesus go,

Saying thus, in Him confiding,
   " Lay thy hands on them and pray,"
His disciples, gently chiding,
   Send the little ones away.
Jesus seeth them from Him driven,
   " Oh! forbid them not," saith He,
" Of such is my kingdom Heaven,
   Suffer them to come to me."

Little infant, type of Heaven,
   Like those little ones of old,
May'st thou, darling, ne'er be driven
   From that gentle Saviour's fold.
May He in thy youth and beauty
   Shield thee with his holy arm,
Teaching thee a Christian's duty,
   Guarding thee from every harm,
And when life's short journey's ended,
   And thine eyes in death grow dim,
May He, pardoning when offended,
   Suffer thee to come to Him.

We, thy loving parents, bless thee,
   And on this thy natal day,
While to our fond hearts we press thee,
   Thus unto that Saviour pray—

" Blessed Saviour, gentle Jesus,
    Who upon those children smiled,
Bless the presents this day given,
    Bless them to our little child ;
Teach her, in the Prayer-book's pages,
    Thou dost hear and answer prayer,
And, in sorrow, let thy Bible
    Teach her to find comfort there."

THE MEETING OF THE JUSTICES.

The Hon'ble G—C——l on the water-supply.

It was an ancient gentleman,
  And he talk'd for hours three,
" By thy long lean form and dismal drone
  We fain must listen to thee."

The town-hall doors are open'd wide,
  " We must be off," quoth they—
He stay'd them only with his hand,
  They let him have his say.

He dazed them with his dismal drone
  Which through them sent a thrill,
They listen'd all respectfully,
  The speaker had his will.

The Justices sat round the board,
  They could not choose but hear,
And for three mortal hours he pour'd
  This subject in their ear—

" Water, water, everywhere,
   Oh, how the tanks do stink !
Water, water, everywhere,
   Nor one clean drop to drink !"

" The ice is here, the ice is there,
   The ice is all around,
And with our frappèd champagne cup
   In little bits is ground,

" All 'neath a hot and copper sky
   Our bread we daily earn,
And for a pleasant drink at noon
   Our parchèd throats do burn.

" And still the cry is everywhere,
   His peg as each one drinks,
And from his nose excludes the air,
   " Oh, how the water stinks !"

" Water, water, everywhere,
   Oh, how the tanks do stink !
Water, water, everywhere,
   Nor one clean drop to drink !"

The Justices sate all dismay'd
   To hear this droning bore,
They would, had they not been afraid,
   Have bolted through the door.

They sate as men who have been stunn'd,
   And are of sense bereft,
Nor did they feel at ease again
   Till that old drone had left.

———

THE " ALABAMA."

One of the London papers commenced an article on the fight between the " Kearsarge" and the " Alabama" with the following rolling hexameter—" Fathoms deep in Norman waters lies the good ship ' Alabama.' "

Fathoms deep in Norman waters lies the good ship
    " Alabama,"
Fell destroyer of the " Hattrass"—Yankee merchant
    ship alarmer,
Burner of a hundred vessels, terror of each Northern
    skipper,
Vanish'd 'mid the depth of ocean lies the dreaded
    Southern clipper.
Shout your pœans, Northern journals, o'er the vanish'd
    " Alabama,"
Semmes and crew, like Moorish Monarch, murmur " Ay
    de mi, Alhama."
But, unlike that Moorish noodle, history this boast will
    wreath them,
That they did not lose their honor, though their vessel
    sank beneath them.

Scourge and dread of Northern commerce, cursed by
    every underwriter,
Loud did Federal cruisers bluster that they only wish'd
    to fight her;
But she roamed the seas at pleasure, their best merchant
    vessels burning,
Caring not a fig for cruisers, all their bosh and bunkum
    spurning;
Till at last the "Kearsarge" caught her, gave her pump-
    kin sauce and smash'd her,
And in several little pieces like a broken egg-shell
    crash'd her;
Stove her sides in, knock'd her fires out, made her decks
    one scene of slaughter,
Till she disappear'd for ever fathoms deep in Norman
    water.
But take care my gentle "Kearsarge," "Vanderbilt,"
    and "Tuscarora,"
Semmes will get a better vessel, of your plated-sides a
    borer,
And he'll let the daylight through you, knock you into
    tarnal shivers,
Sweep you all from off the ocean, from your ports and
    from your rivers.

THE SCREAM OF THE AMERICAN EAGLE,

OR

THE CROW OF YANKEE-DOODLE.

You sneaking skunks of England
  Who stay at home at ease,
Who think because you never fight
  You're rulers of the seas.
Another pirate launch again
  To match a New York foe,
For the fame of your name
  Which has had so sad a blow,
While we Yankees bluster loud and long
  And over England crow
           Cock-a-doodle-doo.

The shatter'd " Alabama "
  Lies deep beneath the wave,
Your finest guns and gunners
  Their vessel couldn't save,
When our noble ship, the " Kearsarge,"
  Her shot and shell did throw,
To the bottom in an hour
  Did the " Alabama " go,

And we Yankees bluster loud and long
And over England crow
Yankee-doodle-doo.

The flag of old Columbia
Shall ne'er again be furl'd
Till, having scourged the Southern States,
We whip the whole wide world ;
With real lightning from our guns
Our thunderbolts we'll throw,
Till not a single Britisher
Upon the seas doth shew,
Then wont we bluster loud and long
And over England crow
Cook-a-doodle-doooo

Yes, then, you sneaking Britishers,
Our song and feast shall flow
When we sink your Island, Queen and all,
Old ocean's depths below,
And masters of the ' varsal airth
We'll liquor to and fro,
Drink gin-slings with our Irish slaves
And trumpets loudly blow
To the fame of our name,
And o'er the whole world crow
Yankee-doodle-doooooo.

MY " COLLEEN BAWN."

"Every night," he said, "I watch that light in my garden, and I remember poor Eily O'Connor's light on Muckross Head, as she watched for Hardress Cregan, and I think of my own Colleen Bawn."

A light used to shine on Muckross Head,
   Which told that the Colleen Bawn
With weary heart and with eyelids red
Sate sighing to hear her husband's tread,
Sate sighing at times till the night had fled
   To end with a drearier morn.

At times he came and her beacon bright
   From that moment ceased its ray,
And the darkness told that her heart was light
That had sigh'd so long for the coming night
And pined, as the moments wing'd their flight,
   For the love which she miss'd by day.

At other times that lamp burn'd on
   But vainly show'd its light,
It shone till the last of the stars was gone,
Till the sun appear'd that beacon shone,
Till poor Eily felt that her watch was done
   With the end of the weary night.

And like that light whose brilliant beams
   Lit Hardress o'er the tide,
My garden lamp all brightly gleams
For her who in my nightly dreams
In all her gentle beauty seems
   To call me to her side.

And still that lamp its part must play,
   And its quivering glimmer shine,
Till the weary eyes that watch its ray
Shall beam with the light of a happier day,
Till a wife's fond love shall find its way
   To this lonely heart of mine.

THE ALBUM AND THE BET.

Little wifey, dull one day, rather seedy too,
  With no parties, balls, or play, having nought to do,
Says, " I'll go to town to-day, and buy something new,"
  And in her own coaxing way gives a kiss or two.

Then, her seediness all gone and her dulness too,
  Strange how shopping doth alone woman's strength
    renew,
Forth she goes to shops well-known, wanders show-
    rooms through,
  And at last, all tired grown, buys this album new.

And when I, my day's work done, once more wifey see,
  She with looks of love and fun shews the book to me,
Bets me kisses two to one, sketch and poetry,
  Ere she sees to-morrow's sun, in this book will be.

Home I've come at half-past five, tired with office work,
  Weary, stupid, and I strive wifey's task to shirk,
But the rain prevents a drive, so she plays the Turk,
  Tells me I must look alive or the bet she'll burk.

So with pencil I commence to concoct a verse,
    Trying with my wandering sense to be clear and terse,
But my silence gives offence, wifey gets perverse,
    Says my lines are all pretence and my conduct worse,

Frowns and pouts her pretty lips, says, " you used to
        write
In that horrid name of Pips, and again you might,"
In my ink the pencil dips, then turns down the light,
    Pinches me with playful nips till I laugh outright.

Then my pen I throw away, much to wife's surprise,
    So at least she seems to say with those knowing eyes,
And with wits all gone astray from the table rise,
    " I have won my bet to-day," laughingly she cries.

But next day the early morn sees the task begun,
    And within three hours of dawn all these lines are
        done,
And the ponies too are drawn, and my bet is won,
    And upon my lips are borne kisses two to one.

IN MEMORIAM.

Sept. 1864.

Poor little baby
  Has gone to his rest,
All sinless and pure
  To his Saviour's breast,
A cherub 'mid millions
  The happy and blest.

Thus prays his lone mother,
  "May Thy will be done,
But, merciful Father,
  When my course is run,
Oh, let me go also
  Where baby is gone."

IN MEMORIAM.

June 1866.

One morning I was lying ill, ah, very, very ill
  And a little darling baby came and nestled in my bed,
And though in pain and torture I felt a happy thrill
  Of heavenly love and pleasure as my little babe I fed.

How lovingly I watch'd her, my tender tiny pet,
   And pray'd to God (how often) not to let my birdie
      fly,
For my heart had even then not been able to forget
   Her buried baby-brother who only lived to die.

And the hours flew by so happily, as daily there I lay
   With my heart so full of yearning to the treasure by
      my side,
Only waiting for the blissful time when at the close of
      day
   I should shew her to her father with all a mother's
      pride.

But a day of sickness came, then a wild and harrowing
      dream
   Of my wee pet baby dying in agony and pain,
Of whispering voices round me, of one heart-breaking
      theme,
   The wan and wasted darling I should never see again.

They told me some time after of the sad baptismal rite,
   Of the signing of the Cross on my dying baby's brow
Ere her sinless soul departed in its early happy flight
   To the bosom of that Saviour where she is nestling
      now.

There let my darling nestle where pain and sorrow
    cease,
  And let me strive with humbled pride to kiss the
    chastening rod,
That when this life is over I too may rest in peace
  With all my dear beloved ones for ever with our God.

THE GREAT RENT CASE.

A LAY OF THE HIGH COURT IN 1865.

DRAMATIS PERSONÆ.

P. COCCUS	*Knight, Chief Justice.*

NORMNUS	
MAWGNOR	
FERUS BARBATUS	} *Barrister Paisne Judges.*
MAK FERSONIUS	

TREVORUS	
LOCCUS	
BAYLIUS	
GLOVA	
STERUS..	
KEMPUS	} *Sudder-Alla, or Sudder Paisne Judges.*
SAMBO NIGER	
CAMBELLUS	
ELFIN JUKSUN	
SUETONIUS KARRUS ..	

PIDDONTONIUS	{ *Crier of the High Court, whose business it is to swear in people, and also to swear at people for making a noise; also to maintain silence, and who does so effectually by kicking all noisy ones out.*

BERNUS RUFUS	{ *Badshahee Vakeels or Attornies of the High Court; also "broken-hearted bachelors, who prolong their weary lives" by residing at the Bengal Club.*
FENNUS	

WATKININIUS .. .. ..⎤
HATCHUS .. .. ⎟
STACCUS .. .. ⎟
COLLIUS .. .. ⎟
AUGUSTUS .. .. ⎬ *Likewise Badshahee Vakeels.*
PALIA LOGUS .. .. .. ⎟
GULIELMUS JUDEX .. ⎟
SIMMUS .. .. ⎟
CARRA-PIETAS.. .. ..⎦

GRAAMUS .. .. *Advocate General.*

EGLINTONIUS .. .. .. { *Barrister, also a broken-hearted bachelor of the Bengal Club.*

JONNI COCRANUS .. ..⎤
DIKKI DOINIUS .. ..⎟
JUCUNDUS PAULUS ..⎬ *Also Barristers.*
CORITONNUS .. .. ..⎦

THE GREAT RENT CASE.

A LAY OF THE HIGH COURT IN THE YEAR MDCCCLXV.

I.

Ho! Nazirs, sound your tom-toms!
  Ho! Sheriff, clear the way!
The Judges ride, in all their pride,
  To the High Court to-day.
To-day the chairs and benches
  Are snatched from room and hall,
And still does Piddontonius
  For chairs more loudly bawl.
Shout! gallant little Crier!
  Your eye-glass tightly fit,
Arrange your splendid Forum
  So every Judge may sit.
Each Judge is robed in sable,
  His gills flow long and wide,
Like Bull-frog in the fable,
  He swells with conscious pride—

While flows the Hooghly River,
  While Ochterlony stands,
The largest monument we have
  On Bengal's sultry lands;

So long will be remember'd
  The dreary great Rent Case,
When fifteen Judges met at once
  With one grave solemn face :
So long will be remember'd,
  Where white or black man treads,
The fifteen solemn Judgments
  Of fifteen learned heads.

———

II.

See how the fifteen Judges
  Come pouring in amain,
In buggy, brougham, and britzka,
  Across the dusty plain.
From all along Chowringhee,
  From far off Theatre Road,
From many a lordly mansion,
  From many a swell abode ;

From Clubs, where hen-peck'd husbands
  Find refuge from their wives,
Where broken-hearted bachelors
  Prolong their weary lives ;

From Beebee Herring's quarters,
    And Mrs. Box's place,
Where mothers teach their daughters
    To flirt with fitting grace—
See how the fifteen Brethren
    Come flocking to the Hall;
See Loceus, short and slender,
    Cambellus, thin and tall;

And there behold P. Coceus,
    The chief of all is he—
P. Coceus of the subtle brain,
    No subtler brain could be.
Of iron nerve and iron brain,
    No labour doth he shirk,
But toils and works, and toils amain,
    And makes the others work.
Their noses to the grinding stone,
    The sweat upon their brow,
The Judges get no holidays,
    No leave of absence now !
Ah ! how they hate P. Coceus,
    Who will not let them go
To sniff the ocean breezes,
    Or climb the hills of snow !

Now rushes in stout Baylius,
　With light and springy tread,
As light as when, in days of old,
　He danced himself to bed.
And here comes dear old Sterus,
　Whose "cannons" are so true,
Who handles his "Joe Manton"
　As deftly as his cue.
Who does not love good Sterus,
　Whose heart, in simple truth,
Shews far less of the Sudder Judge,
　Than of warm-hearted youth?
Now Suetonius Karrus,
　With the fine Roman nose,
Chief ruler of the banquet
　When Scotia's whiskey flows.
A hero, too, at cricket,
　Of Karrus tales are told
How well he kept his wicket,
　In the brave days of old.
And after him comes Trevorus,
　Of gentle blood and mien,
Through all his long career has he
　A " preux chevalier" been,
Then, arm-in-arm with Glova,
　Is Elfin Juksun seen.

Now comes the kindly Normnus,
   Erst acting chief was he,
No greater favorite anywhere
   Than Normnus can be.
Then Mawgnor the handsome,
   And Kempus, grave and glum,
Then, peering through his spectacles,
   Doth Mak Fersonius come.

Ah, here comes Sambo Niger,
   Swarth son of sultry zone,
As proud is he as Lucifer
   Of his Judicial throne—
A sop to the Bengallee,
   To English minds a wrench,
Our rulers thought it right to raise
   One Native to the Bench.
Brown Hindustanee maidens,
   While listening to the sighs
Of Young Bengal, repeat the tale
   Of Sambo Niger's rise—
And minstrels at the nautches,
   Where young men take their fling,
To Rajahs and to Rances,
   Of Sambo's tullub sing.
Now, making up the number,
   Though last not least is he,

With sparkling eyes and big black beard,
  Ferus Barbatus see.
Of all those fifteen Brethren,
  For wisdon far renown'd,
Ferus Barbatus was the last
  Who came from English ground.
What though of all the junior,
  Though last not least is he ;
The only Judge who wears a beard—
  Ferus Barbatus see !

III.

Now gather'd in the Forum,
  The fifteen Brethren meet,
And Sheriff Collius marshals each
  To his appointed seat.

P. Coccus and the Seniors
  Above make lordly show,
While Ferus and the Juniors
  Are ranged in line below.
Two goodly rows of Judges !
  So fine a sight, I ween,

Of talent such a grand array
  Is very rarely seen.
And while the fifteen Brethren
  Are sitting there in State,
And to each other whispering
  And holding short debate,
Before they give their judgments,
  We'll turn, and for a space
Look on the crowd who gather round
  To hear the great Rent Case.
Here mingle swell Attornies
  With members of the Bar,
And swarthy Native pleaders,
  And many a zemindar.
From every town and district
  Which boasts the smallest Court ;
From paddy fields and jungle
  Where snakes and jackals sport ;
From talook and from village
  Where naked urchins play ;
From hut and from cutcherry
  Where suitors bribe their way ;
From where the dirty buffaloes
  Through muddy marshes roam,
As greasy and as dirty
  As baboos are at home ;

From many a " country garden,"
   From many a city slum—
To hear the Rent Case judgments
   The swarthy Natives come.
Now see those Arian lawyers,
   Attornies and their clerks,
Who at the fifteen Brethren
   Pass "jocative" remarks,
While each of them is thinking
   With envy and with grief,
Of what his bill of costs had been
   For each tremendous brief,
Had his old " family Idol,"
   With oil and paint begrim,
Been only good enough to send
   The great Rent Case to him.
But, ah! whose grand red whiskers,
   All fiery and a-glow,
Are with the punkah waving,
   So gently to and fro?
They point out Bernus Rufus;
   Full proud is he, I ween,
Of his Dundreary whiskers,
   And of their ruddy sheen.
And there see Watkininius,
   The lord of Airy Hall,

Talking to Pallia-Logus
   With most provoking drawl;
For Pallia-Logus longs
   To tell (so says his face)
Some story of his wrongs
   Some injured client's case.
Ah, learned Watkininius,
   If quickly feather'd nest
Were proof of far superior brain
   How well you'd stand the test !
Oft hath blind fortune smiled,
   With Buxis and Bequest
On you, her favorite child,
   While frowning on the rest.
There, too, impulsive Fennus,
   Of whom the words are true,
" You cannot know good Fennus,
   And fail to like him, too."
Near him stands long grey Staccus,
   A Barrister erewhile,
And Collins and Augustus,
   All sons of Erin's isle.
Now, bursting with importance,
   The learned Hatchus see,
With Act viii at his fingers' ends,—
   A ready help is he ;

On every puzzling motion,
  Or difficult decree,
Hatchus is ever to the front,
  Amicus curiæ!
There Gulielmus Judex,
  A veteran grey and pale,
Takes Simmus by the button-hole
  And tells some ancient tale
Of what we did in former days
  When Ryan was our Chief,
And how since those good days of yore
  All things have come to grief.
Here Jew-loved Carra-Pietas,
  Armenia's gifted son,
Advises that old dirty Jew
  Of business to be done.
Then he and Piddontonius,
  (Oh, but they've stomachs tough !)
Take from that greasy Hebrew
  A pinch of Jewish snuff.
Near them see wan Gillandus.
  A good man, but so spare,
You'd think that a musquito's breath
  Would waft him into air.
There Graamus, with his calm pale face,
  With Eglintonius sits,

And whispers something now and then,
  And picks his brief to bits.
And bustling Corritonnus
  His eager fingers flips
To the " Englishman's" chuprassee
  In waiting for the 'slips.'
And dear old Jonni Cocranus—
  Whose heart, as good as gold,
Still bears him up right manfully,
  As in the days of old—
Sits twirling round his spectacles,
  And, from his numerous store,
Tells to his laughing listeners
  Some anecdote of yore.
There, too, Jucundus Paulus,
  With ever ready jest,
Cracks jokes with Dikki Doinius,
  Of all the Bar the best,
Who, whether at the festive board
  Or in forensic hall,
For many years has proved himself
  The leader of them all.
But now the fifteen Brethren
  Have closed their short debate,
And each sits grim and solemn
  And shakes his learned pate.

Now fit your eye-glass, Crier!
Now "Silence!" loudly shout,
Then tumble from your little desk
And kick the rabble out!

IV.

Then first his judgment Trevorus
  Read out in language clear,
And such a silence then was kept
  A pin's drop you might hear.
He cited many authors
  As ancient as the hills,
And quoted from the history
  Of India by Mills—
From long forgotten statutes
  Read many a dreary line,
Which seemed to unprofessionals
  Like throwing pearls to swine—
Read Menu's regulations,
  And many a puzzling clause,
And long and dismal doctrines
  About the old rent laws.
Of *pykhast* and of *koodkhast* ryots
  The difference did define,

And pointed out the bearing of
    Act X. of '59—
Read the decennial settlement,
    And minutes by John Shore,
The laws of ancient Soubahs,
    And Heaven knows what more!
At last, when all grew weary,
    And sleep proclaim'd her reign,
Great Trevorus thought 'twas time enough
    To close the lengthen'd strain.
And this is how that learned Judge
    The Rent Case did decide—
He settled that a tenant
    Who twelve years should abide
Upon his landlord's property
    Should have an owner's right
To share the rent—and landlord
    Should get it as he might.
Then Trevorus nudged stout Baylius,
    Who'd been an hour asleep,
And Baylius so pinch'd Loceus
    As made his flesh to creep.
And Loceus, Baylius, Glova,
    Confirming the decree,
Said—"With our learned Brother
    We all of us agree."

And Elfin Juksun said the same,
  And with a gentle shake
Caused snoozing Mak Fersonius
  From slumber to awake.
Then out spake Mak Fersonius
  Of imposts and *abwabs*,
Of *nirrikbundy* tenures,
  Kubooleuts and *Kincobs*—
And used such wondrous language'
  That gentle sleep again
Of every tortured listener
  O'ercame the weary brain ;
When suddenly he finish'd—
  " With very slight demur,
With learned Brother Trevorus
  In substance I concur."
Then spake Barbatus Ferus,
  Not once asleep was he,
But through it all was wide awake,
  As learned Judge should be ;
And first, like Judge at Westminster,
  The facts he did relate,
The judgment of the lower Court,
  The questions in debate—
Then sifted points of evidence,
  Doubted if facts were clear,

Discuss'd some learned questions
   Which no one cared to hear—
Said—" Many loose admissions
   Throughout this cause I trace,
Which never would have been allow'd
   Had I but tried the case ;"
And added :—" Into regions
   (Where I am not at home)
Of novel legislation
   We're here required to roam.
The learned Courts of Westminster
   Ne'er go beyond the case,
'Gainst travelling from the issue
   They ever set their face,
But in this curious country
   We travel far beyond
The issue, till we tumble in
   The slough of sheer despond !
And 'tis so in this instance,
   We cannot help ourselves ;
So I have run through all the books
   Which ornament my shelves—
And this important subject
   Has met with at my hands
That long and grave attention
   Which such a case demands."

Then argued he the matter
    For half an hour and more,
And sleep again proclaim'd her reign,
    And men were heard to snore.
But every earthly thing must end,
    All dreary though it be,
And Ferus was at last wound up,
    And this was his decree—
" While my decision with the rest
    Will, in the main, agree,
My Brethren's notions, I confess,
    Have not assisted me ;
And as it never is my rule,
    Without some grave demur,
With any other learned Judge
    Entirely to concur ;
So now, though partly I dissent,
    I, on the whole, agree
With all those learned Judges
    Who have preceded me."
Then with a voice sonorous
    Cambellus had his say,
And lethargy came o'er us,
    Throughout that weary day.
" Spare us ! Cambellus, spare us,"
    Was oft the mutter'd cry,

As still he went on reading,
  And still the hours went by.
But mortal is Cambellus,
  He, too, wound up at last,
And with the others did concur,
  And his decree was pass'd.
After Cambellus, Sambo,
  Great Sambo Niger, came,
And, following in his Brethren's wake,
  His ruling was the same.
Then Mawgnor the handsome,
  Then Kempus, glum and grave,
And Normnus, the kind and good,
  The same decision gave.
'Twould be a weary business,
  'Twould take a day to tell
The stores of legal wisdom
  That from those Brethren fell.
Then, having roused himself from sleep,
  Sterus took up the cue,
And, with a few remarks in point,
  Agreed with Trevorus too—
" Now yield thee, great P. Coccus,
  Now yield with proper grace,
And join with us in one decree
  In this important case."

Thus spake his learned Brethren,
   And all the crowd awoke,
When up rose great P. Coccus
   And thus the silence broke :—
" I must confess, in all I've heard
   From all my great compeers,
I have not heard one single word
   To change my own ideas,
Or alter in the least degree
   Opinions I express'd,
When, in the case of Ishur Ghose,
   I differ'd from the rest.
I'll add that in sincerity
   Most wanting I should be,
If, for the sake of courtesy,
   I now with them agree ;
Or for a moment were to say
   I entertain a doubt,
From anything I've heard to-day,
   That I am right throughout."
Then went he through his reasons,
   But long before he'd done
The crowd had all departed,
   The Judges were alone !
And Piddontonius gently fell
   Into a state of doze,

Now scratching of his forehead,
  Now fingering his nose.
And soon it was throughout the town
  By all the people known
That in the Rent Case judgments
  P. Coccus was alone !

V.

All through the dull hot weather,
  When the Nor'-Westers blow,
And down the throat the mango-fish
  With simkin glibly go—
When in his fine verandah
  The money-making swell
Sits chatting with the pretty wife,
  The wife he loves so well—
And through the bright cold season,
  And through the wretched rains,
In country, town, and village,
  O'er all these dreary plains,
When the chandeliers shine brightly
  Or the small chirag is lit,

And when about our gardens
   The little fireflies flit—
In Court and in Cutcherry
   Where Bar and Judges strut,
In Club and lordly mansion,
   In dwelling-house and hut,
When jackals howl around us,
   And the musquito's hum
Tells that a much more worrying brute
   To bother us has come—
At dances and at nautches,
   'Mid halls of dazzling light,
At weary burra khanas,
   Or Christy Minstrels' night—
Of the great Rent Case the story
   Full often will be told,
How Judge P. Coccus stood alone,
   By all his Brethren sold !

THE CALCUTTA RACE-COURSE.

PAST AND PRESENT.

"Come, good friend Pips, now tell us," said Charlie
    Hart to me,
As we waited in the Stewards' Stand the hurdle-race
    to see,
"Say, who's that tall grey-headed man full higher by
    a head
Than any six-foot man I see, there standing by the
    shed ?"

That son of Anak, Charlie, is the Nestor of our turf,
Whose iron frame still laughs at time as rocks defy the
    surf,
A glance at him recalls the sport of many a year ago,
When Elepoo came thundering by like arrow from a
    bow.

That fine old sportsman, Charlie, the fearful crash did
    see,
When the English horse "Lieutenant" and the Arab
    "Absentee"

Were neck and neck together and the loose horse 'gainst
    them tore
And " Lieutenant's" jockey, Hardy, was thrown to rise
    no more.*

He can tell you of the time when the great Fieschi ran,
And Robert Ross, in green and white, was ever in the
    van—
Of five close heats he once saw run by Crab and Oran-
    more,
The gamest struggle ever seen upon a course before.†

He could tell you of the wondrous stride of his own
    Elepoo,
The tallest, fastest Arab Calcutta ever knew—
There were good horses in those days, as he can well
    recall,
But Barker upon Elepoo, hands down, shot by them all!

---

    * The two horses were racing together when the loose horse ran
against them and the whole three came to the ground with frightful
violence—Hardy was kill'd on the spot—"Lieutenant" was so much
injured that he was at once shot—and I do not think 'Absentee' ever
gallop'd again.
    † Crab and Oranmore—two Arabs—ran five heats—each winning
one, and there being two dead heats, they were obliged to run the fifth
heat, which Crab won.

And talking thus of Mr. Jones,* I saw with dreamy eye
Upon the old Calcutta Course a string of nags go by—
There Corriemonie gallop'd past with Frampton on his
   back,
And long thin Hall and Sweetlips tore like mad upon
   their track.

And Gash, that cruel punisher, when on a jaded horse,
(Few men could ply both whip and spur with such
   tremendous force)
Went pounding by on Snowball, the pet of Hardwick's
   stud,†
And with him steady Roostum steer'd a colt of desert
   blood

Then the Island-Childe and Minuet, Crab, Glaucus,
   Boomerang,
Sent the dust all flying round them as to the spur they
   sprang,
Next Evans upon Wahaby, and Barker on boy Jones
Of two raw-bony Walers " made no especial bones"‡—

---

* Mr. Jones—the racing cognomen of Elepoo's owner.
   † Gash came to a dreadful end in Jessore or Kishnaghur. He was
riding home one night when he was very drunk. He fell from his
horse, and in his helpless state was killed and half-eaten by jackals.
   ‡ Barker said, on one occasion when he was ask'd about two Walers
he had to ride against, " well, Sir, I don't know, but I will make no
special bones of THEM."

Then the gallant chesnut Selim, the first of Waler
    fame,
Passing everything before him, like a flash of lightning
    came—
And rattling fast behind him with Joy upon his
    back
Came Mr. Charles' Ishmael, another Derby crack.

But now the hurdle-race begins and my short dream
    is o'er,
And when the race is o'er friend Charlie asks once
    more—
" Say, Pips, who is that tall thin man with grey hair
    on his brow,
There trotting by on that bay horse, who started them
    just now ?"

That fine tall fellow, Charlie, has been starter here for
    years,
And his management of Course and Stand his name
    to us endears,
And for his sake we're glad to think that Wallace
    leaves us soon
To find new health and strength among the braes of
    Bonnie Doon.

He'll tell you how the Country-breds, seen on this course
   no more,
Could carry in the days of old their colors to the fore,
He'll tell you, no man better, how to rear and keep a
   stud
Of Arabs, Walers, Country-breds, or any kind of blood.

With sportsman's pleasure he recalls his chesnut mare,
   Grace Lee,
Who won the great Colonial in the season—fifty-three,
And how his mare, Meg Merrilies, in the season—
   fifty-eight
And fifty-nine, and following year, bore off the Mer-
   chants' Plate—

" Now who is he who saunters by as fresh as morning air,
And nods to every passer-by, so cool, so debonair,
So closely shaved, so well got up, now who may that
   man be ?"
Thus Charlie Hart with curious look did once more
   question me.

" To see that man and not know him argues yourself
   unknown,
As good a chap as ever breathed, a sportsman to the
   bone,

Who takes the ups and downs of life without a thought
    of care,
At Club, or Race-course, social board, a favourite every-
    where—

No heartier welcome ever rang on winning owner's ears
Than that thrice echo'd welcome when the welkin rang
    with cheers,
When ' Famine' won the Derby in eighteen fifty-two,
And cheers went up for Famine and Charlie Marten too!"

" Now once more, Pips, forget the past, and tell us who
    they be
Who stand among the horses there collected round that
    tree ?"
I turn'd and look'd, and Monty stood amid his Arab
    pets
And with friend Pritchard shew'd their points to two
    admiring Vets.

And happy as a king he'll be that sportsman good as
    gold,
(Altho' it seems hard lines to him that Hermit should
    grow old)
If he can only hit upon some little Arab pet
That will answer all his yearnings and win the Derby yet.

And see that tall good-looking man, a soldier every inch,
Who from the trench, the fight, the march, was never
      known to flinch,
At Inkerman's stern " soldiers' fight," on Delhi's blood-
      stain'd plain,
As cool as on the cricket-ground was ever Seymour Blane.

In the receipt of Customs friend Crawford long has been
A first-rate man in office, a sportsman true and keen
Whose quick unerring eye can spot the winner by a nose,
And from whose honest heart no thought save that of
      honor flows.

And with them stands a well-known son of Sligo's
      lordly line
Whose well-earn'd fame 'mongst sporting men requires
      no praise of mine.
And naming him the Stewards' list* I've closed—and for
      to-day
I think that for the " Sporting Mag." I've done enough,
      you'll say.

---

* Stewards in 1866—Beckwith (*i. e.* 'Mr. Jones'), Wallace, Crawford
Marten, Monty Turnbull, Lord Ulick Browne, and Col. Blane.

" WRITE, SPORTSMEN, WRITE."

Written for the 'Oriental Sporting Magazine.'

Write, gallant sportsman, write
    Of the sport which you have seen,
Let the fun you've witness'd see the light
    In the " Sporting Magazine."

Write of that rattling burst
    When the jackall broke away
At such a pace from the first
    That few of the nags could stay.
Tell us, how pump'd of breath,
    Your Arab terribly blown,
You flounder'd in at the death
    Yourself and the huntsman alone.

Tell of the tiger's roar
    As he bounded into " the clear,"
Of the twenty bullets and more
    That stopp'd his wild career;
Or write of the charging boar
    Which flush'd your maiden spear,
As you rode with three or four
    Without a thought of fear.

Let's hear of that buffalo ride
  When you rode the big bull to a stand,
After chasing him stride for stride
  Over miles of broken land,
Of each shot that crash'd through his side
  And dyed with blood the strand,
How he reel'd, and fell, and died
  A prey to a sportsman's hand.

Or tell of that 'mugger' fierce,
  The terror of all around,
Whose sides no bullet could pierce
  Till you appear'd on the ground;
How your small exploding shell
  Went bang from its rifled bore,
And burst in his side so well—
  That " mugger" was fear'd no more.

Let us hear of that glorious sport,
  The elephant hunt on foot,
Where nature's great lesson is taught—
  The triumph of man o'er the brute;
Or tell us some story of Home
  When after a wearisome " cram,"
You have steer'd a swift yacht through the foam
  Or pull'd a stroke oar on the Cam.

Or write of the wicket kept
    Till a hundred and ten were scored,
And how the slow twister crept
    Into stumps not easily floor'd ;
Or tell how the snipe went down
    To the tune of forty brace,
And how you carn'd the renown
    Of being " best shot" in the place.

Or tell of that triumph of nerve
    When you held the young Waler so straight,
That in spite all his dodges to swerve
    You rode him clean over the gate ;
Or send an account of the race
    When your game little Arab was pass'd,
After going all round at a pace
    At which Hermit himself couldn't last.

Or narrate us some wonderful luck,
    When out after wild duck or goose,
You brought down a jolly black buck
    As big as a Canada moose ;
Or write of the grouse on the moors,
    Of the great antler'd king of the glen,
Of your lion hunt out with the boors
    When you bearded the beast in his den ;

Or tell of your race-meeting ball,
    Of the picnic the following day,
Of the stroll round the great waterfall,
    Where the girls had it all their own way :
Aye, write of the eyes whose bright beams
    Went straight to your heart with such power
That all your day thoughts and your dreams
    Have been of those eyes since that hour.

Or write of that growling old bear
    Which bolted straight out of the bush,
(When the beaters discover'd his lair)
    And came down the hill with a rush ;
How, when only half-way down the hill
    On his hind legs a moment he stood,
You sent him an opening pill
    Which sto₁p'd all his growling for good.

Come tell us some story of pluck,
    Of steadiness, patience, or skill,
Of games won by science or luck—
    Of anything else that you will ;
Of the triumphs of rod or of gun,
    Of saddle, oar, bat, or of spear,
Even give us some story of fun
    For fun is a welcome guest here.

THE GREAT DURBAR.

A Modern Lay.

I.

Jan Larrens of Calcutta,
  Chief Knight of India's Star,
Has sworn by all the Hindoo gods
  He'll hold a Grand Durbar.
By Gunga's stream he swore it
  And named at once the day,
Then bade his Aides-de-Camp go forth,
East, and west, and south, and north,
  To summon the array.

East, and west, and south, and north,
  The Aides-de-Camp ride fast;
All over Upper India
  Their summonses are cast.
Kennedius spurs his chesnut,
  Lokwodius crams his grey,
Randalius cheers his Arab on
  All through the livelong day.

See how the perspiration
  Pours down Kennedius' face !
It trickles o'er his bran-new coat
  And damages the lace.
And still he gallops onward,
  Nor halts except to beg
The way to some great Rajah's hold,
  Or else to get a peg.

North, and south, and east, and west,
  Like couriers bold they ride,
And with Jan Larrens' summonses
  They scour the country wide.
Shame on each sulky Rajah
  Who hides himself afar;
Who stays among his dancing girls,
And, warrior there, all fiercely twirls
His black moustache in warlike curls,
  And laughs at the Durbar.

And now the loyal chieftains
  Are pouring in amain,
And noise and dust are rampant
  On Agra's sun-burnt plain.
Cream-coloured horses amble by,
  And painted tattoos prance,

Spur'd on by Maharajahs bold,
In blue and silver, green and gold,
With Cashmere shawls in many a fold,
And jewels rare of price untold,—
And arm'd, as were their sires of old,
  With matchlock, sword, and lance;
  And all around in wondering trance
Upon " Barbaric pearl and gold"
  The English eye may glance.

The horsemen and the footmen
  Are gathering fast around,
And elephants and camels
  Swarm thickly o'er the ground.
Tagrag and bobtail everywhere
  Half wild from heat and bhang,
And horses with their trappings rare
Of tigers' skins and tufts of hair,
And men resplendent in the glare
Of rainbow-colour'd satin, share
The wondering gaze and furious stare
Of many an Anglo-Saxon there;
The while, all through the startled air,
  The noisy tom-toms clang.

See on yon dirty camel
  A Rajah so obese,

He looks as though he ne'er was fed
 On aught save ghee and grease;
And on that sleepy elephant,
 Cross-legg'd, and, oh, so fat,
Two sirdars roll like porpoises,
 Now this side, now on that.

Again, on that white charger
 Painted with spots of red
With mane and tail all scarlet
 Red plumes upon his head :
Squeezed in by panting footmen,
 Clinging to tail and sides,
There goes some swell with legs so thin
So wondrous straight from hip to shin,
That each would answer for a pin,
And yet 'twould be almost a sin
To greet that warrior with a grin,
 So scornfully he rides.

And there a big Paharry,
 Swollen with rage and pride,
Who cannot sit upright or straight,
His elephant's unwieldy gait
 Rolls him from side to side.
And on a camel trotting by,
All pale his cheek and wild his eye,

Now bump'd below, now toss'd up high,
With fright his very blood is dry,
   A Rajah from Bhopal;
And in a bullock-bandy drives,
Surrounded by her sister wives,
   His dusky Noormahal.

From far off Central India,
   Where Tantia Topee fought;
From many a sandy district,
   From many a stony ghaut;
From the land of the five rivers,
   From the gardens of Cashmere,
From many a bower of roses
   On the banks of Bendemeer.

From Joudhpore's sunny regions,
   From Ulwar and Marwar,
From Rajpootana's deserts,
   From Bhurtpore and Narwar;
Pathan, and Jat, and Rajpoot,
   And Jogee from Hurdwar;
The swaggering Sikh, the Chief from Oude;
All shouting, bawling, talking loud,
Hindu and Moslem swell the crowd
   To join the great Durbar.

Even from hot Calcutta
  The oily Rajahs come,
And as they pass you shut your nose
  With finger and with thumb;
And noisier still and noisier
  The thronging crowd becomes—
And louder still and still more loud
  The tom-toms, horns, and drums,
As to the spot where lies his tent,
  Each swarthy chieftain comes.

And at the Railway Station,
  'Midst goods heap'd pile on pile,
Are crowds of Anglo-Saxons
  Half-dead from dust and bile.
There beggar jostles gentle,
  There haut-ton and canaille,
The lower class, the upper crust,
The swindler, and the dealer just,
The man who swells about on trust,
The "cove as wants his luggage fust,"
The swell whose carpet bag is bust,
All yield to smoke, and heat, and dust,
And find that to "get on" they must
  All fraternise awhile.

So through the streets of Agra
  Are tumult, dust, and noise,
A surging tide of restless men
  Of women and of boys.
And all along the Jumna,
  On both banks, near and far,
Flock in the crowds at Indian fairs,
The boothmen with their tawdry wares,
The monkeys, fakirs, dancing bears,
And Dick-po conjurers in pairs,
With strings of cast-off stud-bred mares,
  Come to the great Durbar.

Now all through Agra's city,
  O'er all her suburbs round,
No empty house or tent is seen,
  Nor one clear spot of ground.
Within, without, for miles about,
  'Tis one vast close array,—
A proud man is Jan Larrens
  Upon the Durbar day.

II.

Now, guns, boom forth your welcome ;
　Now, soldiers, clear the way ;
Rajahs will come with beat of drum
　To the Durbar to-day.

Truly a wondrous gathering
　Doth Agra see to-day
Of India's best and bravest chiefs
　Who own Victoria's sway.
All flocking to the tented camp
　Where England's banner flies,
Where great Jan Larrens will receive
　His subjects and allies.

There gleaming in the sunlight,
　Which evermore doth flash
On gold and silver, brass and steel,
　Ten thousand horsemen dash.
Their leaders in chain armour,
　And silks of many a fold,
With sabre, spear, and shield appear,
　Like Saracens of old.

And long, long lines of footmen
   Whole regiments reveal,
Above whose heads the bayonets
   Glisten in waves of steel.

Tall are the fierce wild elephants
   That roam through Oude's Terai,
But taller far the tuskers
   That here come trooping by,—
Proud of their gorgeous trappings,
   Proud of this show and state,
Proud of their ivory howdahs,
   And of their royal freight.

And splendid too the donkeys,
   The zebras, asses, mules,
You see all over Egypt
   Where'er the Pacha rules.
But finer are the asses
   The Prophet's followers ride,
Which pick their way throughout the day
Through all this crowded close array,
With switching tail and nasal bray,
   From morn to eventide.

Here scores of silver tonjons
  Are borne by dusky slaves,
Surrounded by a shouting train,
  With flags and silver staves.
While o'er each silver tonjon
  A gold umbrella gleams,
And fans of silver, waved inside,
  Flash back the sun's bright beams.

Grand are the hunchback'd camels
  That plod to Mecca's shrine,
Or bring through Affghan passes
  Their loads of fruit and wine.
But Mecca's weary pilgrims
  Must go on foot this year,
And caravans must wait awhile,
Though wares are ready, pile on pile,
Ere they can creep in lengthen'd file,
For many a day, for many a mile,
O'er mountain pass, through grim defile,—
  The camels all are here.
All jauntily they trot along
  With noses high and proud;
Their silver bells upon the air
  Ring merrily and loud.

Far as the eye can wander,
  Far as the sight can go,
Are gold and silver everywhere,
Banners, flags, streamers, in the air,
  And weapons bright below.

So through and all round Agra,
  From suburbs near and far,
With clash of cymbal, horn, and drum,
With a vast crowd's discordant hum,
The swarthy chiefs and followers come
To the great Camp where, grim and glum,
  Jan Larrens holds Durbar.

III.

Within a large wide street of tents
  A centre tent is spread,
Which shines conspicuous of them all
  In brilliant folds of red.
And scarlet-coated jemadars
  Rush wildly to and fro ;
And England's banner floats above
  Where sentries pace below.

A lofty shameeana
  Leads to the royal tent,
Through which long rows of flowers
  Diffuse a grateful scent.
There, too, the guard of honour
  And English troopers stand,
And sweet soul-stirring music
  Steals from the Rifles' band.

Outside, grim sons of Anak
  Stiff in their saddles sit,
Each war-horse like a statue stands
  Nor scarcely champs his bit.
Well may the Saxon lounger
  Stay here awhile and gaze,
With swelling heart and kindling eye,
  On England's noble " Bays."

Beyond, for nearly half a mile,
  Extends the " thin red line"
Of British troops, above whose heads
  The glistening bayonets shine ;
And at the end, on either side
  Of that long soldier street,
Big guns are ranged in readiness
  The loyal chiefs to greet.

Upon a golden dais
 Within the royal tent
Is placed a throne on which rupees
 By thousands have been spent.
A kinkhob draped above it,
 All bright with golden sheen,—
That throne is for the Viceroy
 Of mighty England's Queen.

And in a semicircle,
 On both sides of the throne,
Are soft red-cushion'd chairs of state
 Reserved for Chiefs alone.
Next these appear the Governors,
 Jan Larrens' satraps true,
Who seem uneasy in their minds,
 As great men often do.
There sits the stalwart Governor
 Of Bengal's sensual race,
And lines of care and trouble
 Furrow his calm pale face.
Next them the High Court Judges,—
 Whom most do girls admire,
Those who are dress'd in scarlet robes
 Or those in Court attire ?

There Gulielmus Vindex,
　　The C.-in-C., reclines,
So jealous of his pickles,
　　His mutton, and his wines.
Even now may be he's thinking
　　Of sauces, fruits, and jams,
Which disappear'd like winking
　　With potted meats and hams.
When Jervis was his butler,
　　As Aides-de-Camp must be,
Who on the staff of such a chief
　　Themselves may wish to see.

And next the grave Politicals,
　　With wan and anxious air,
Who seem to look as though they wou'd
　　Much rather not be there,
And Secretaries wearing swords
　　They know not how to wear.
Beyond, most pleasant sight of all,
　　Are English ladies seen,
Clothed like a gorgeous flower-bed
　　In every hue and sheen.
Gay is the Doorga Poojah,
　　The Bukree Eed is gay,

But this Durbar will be by far
All India's brightest day.

And now a booming salvo,
    A loud crash from the band,
And in the shameeana
    Scindia is seen to stand.
At once a grave official
    Sinks down on bended knee
And to that haughty chieftain
    Offers a bowl of ghee.
Then doth a swell in new court-dress
    And sword and lace and ruff,
With bow and scrape and courtly speech,
    Hand him a pinch of snuff.

Another stiff Political,
    Of courteous mien and air,
Leads Scindia through the royal tent,
    And seats him in his chair.
And gracefully Kennedius,
    As agile as a fawn,
Glides quickly up and gives the Chief
    His atta and his pawn.

Again a crash of music,
   And 'mid the joyous din,
Jeypore's great Rajah, quaintly dress'd,
   Is likewise ushered in.
The ladies raise their wondering eyes,
   "Sure never man was seen,
With legs so like two walking sticks,
   And such a crinoline!"
Painful are his attempts to walk
   With dignity and grace,
As with that loop'd-up mass in front
   He waddles to his place.
And hard Randalius finds it
   To look demure the while
He sprinkles atta o'er the Chief
And sees him chew the fresh pawn-leaf,
Then with a sigh of deep relief
   He turns away to smile.

Another thin-legg'd Chieftain
   Doth presently appear,
Swathed round in folds of crinoline,
Whose wondrous legs, so long and lean,
Are cased in pants of satin green;
And in that swaggering Chief is seen
   A Rajah from Ajmere.

To him two willing Aides-de-Camp
 Offer, with courtly bow,
Two nicely wrapp'd-up bits of pawn—
 And red as Ocean's scarlet spawn,
Aye, redder than red lobster-prawn,
 Are Ajmere's white teeth now,
And swollen is his whisker'd cheek
 On each side of his face;
Vainly his thanks he tries to speak
While those two Aides-de-Camp, so meek,
 Conduct him to his place.

But, hark, a whisper runs along—
 " A lady in the hall!"
And there in all her beauty stands
 The Begum of Bhopal.
To her do two officials
 Offer on bended knee,
Two silver salvers loaded
 With sweetmeats, dhall, and ghee.
Sweet was the barley-sugar
 And good the Boney's ribs
We got at school when youngsters
 By saving up our dibs.
But sweeter are the condiments,
 Aye, nicer far than all,

With which that day Jan Larrens fed
  The Begum of Bhopal!
Then do two great Politicals,—
  Ah, 'twas a merry sight,—
Kiss both cheeks of the Begum,
  The left cheek and the right.
Then arm-in-arm they lead her
  And place her in her chair,
And smooth her rumpled petticoats
  While she smooths down her hair.
And finally Lokwodius,
  With homage in his eyes,
Unto that noble Begum
  Atta and pawn supplies.
And Bhopal's teeth are scarlet now,
  Her pouting lips are red,—
Red as those gorgeous hues that we
May trace 'neath Oman's glittering sea,
  Above each coral bed!

And thus the Chieftains gather,
  And thus the time is spent,
Till all who have admittance
  Are ranged within the tent.
And then throughout the tent no sound
  Upon the air is borne,

Save the whispering of the ladies,
    The chewing of the pawn.

And now a royal salvo,
    And bands are played and trumpets peal'd,
And at the entrance of the tent
    Jan Larrens stands reveal'd.
Slowly he paces to the throne
    And for a while sits down,
His careworn forehead now unbent,
    Now changing to a frown;
Then, when the bands have ceased to play,
    He stands erect and proud,
And, turning to the chiefs, doth say,
    In language clear and loud,—

" Rajahs and Chiefs, you're welcome here;
    In me your Queen you see:
She bids me offer royal cheer
    To all who loyal be.
My swarthy friends, improve your codes,
    And through your own domains
Dig wells, build schools, make pucka roads,
    And irrigate your plains.

In olden days your sires were rude,
　Your countries torn by strife,
Your laws unjust, your customs crude,
　Your lands with pillage rife.
But now you're under one great Queen,
　One wise and peaceful rule,
And he who would my smiles obtain
　Must drop the olden school.
You've time in plenty, money too:
　Be good and peaceful now,
And try your people's love to share
By mingling with them everywhere,
Their happiness your constant care,
And soon a worthier name you'll bear,
Worthy of that old Patriarch there,
　The hoary Satamow."

This speech delivered—Scindia stands,
　With haughty looks, alone,
And, bowing to Jan Larrens, hands
　An offering to the throne—
Ten bright and newly-coin'd gold mohurs
　In bits of satin rolled,
Jan Larrens taps the profferr'd gift,
　Then hands him back his gold,

And gives him two fine elephants
  Of wondrous height and strength,
Each with a pair of ivory tusks
  Full twenty feet in length;
A pair of milk-white horses
  Bespotted red and blue;
And fifty trays of sweetmeats
  And gems of every hue.
Then o'er the Maharajah throws
  In many a graceful fold,
A robe of satin velvet
  All glittering with gold.

Jeypore comes next, and does the same,
  And meets the same return;
How easily do Native Chiefs
  Their much loved presents earn.
But some, alas! are far too poor,
  And from their squander'd store
They cannot, scrape howe'er they may,
  Give more than one gold mohur.
Yet these are treated handsomely,
  For by all Durbar rules,
A chief who offers one gold mohur
  Gets back a pair of mules.

Y

Now, leaning on Kennedius' arm,
  The Begum of Bhopal
Presents her humble nuzzur
  And smiles upon them all.
Jan Larrens doth that nuzzur touch
  With soft respectful tap,
Then trinkets by the dozen
  He pours into her lap.
Gives her two noble elephants,
  Two horses spotted green,
And hands her with the khillut
  A handsome crinoline!

Ah, why doth bold Kennedius
  With such wild frenzy start?
A thrill of maddening passion
  Shoots to his youthful heart,
As on his arms that Indian Queen
So pleased, so lovingly, doth lean,
While o'er her robes of gold and green
Sways to and fro the crinoline.
Oh, sorrowful the task hath been
To draw a veil o'er that sad scene,—
  To stay the pen, to hush the tongue,
  O'er blighted hopes in one so young!

Ah! who can write of lover's tears?
  Slowly he leads her to her chair,
  Then with one long bewildering stare
He turns and disappears.

When all are thus presented,
  And all have gifts received,
Jan Larrens' weary face begins
  To look somewhat relieved.
He rises from his velvet throne
  And cavalierly trips
To where the Begum in her chair
Sits cross-legg'd with a weary air,
  And sweet jelaibee sips.
Then hands her gently to the floor,
And bowing like a troubadour
Or gallant knight in days of yore,
  Salutes her scarlet lips.
Then as a parting compliment
  To Scindia and Bhopal,
He hands to each a fresh pawn-leaf
And leaves the tented hall.

Again the bands all loudly crash,
  Again the big guns roar,

The glistening bayonets brightly flash,
Like spirits wild the troopers rash
O'er crowds of footmen wildly dash,
And 'mid a dreadful noisy smash
   The big Durbar is o'er.

And through the heat of summer,
   Warm night and sultry day,
While Brahmins teach the girls to love
   And Hindu youths to pray;
When, through the Rajah's palace,
   Or in the poor man's hut,
Against the winds of winter
   The doors are closely shut;
When in his close Zenana
   The Indian swell reclines,
And smokes the bubbling hookah
   And quaffs forbidden wines;
And when in dufter-khanah
   Lall-puggree counts the gains
He made from swarthy Chieftains
   On Agra's sun-burnt plains;
When the ryot drives the bullock,
   And twists his broken tail;
When Hindu maidens seek their loves,
   And old crones fiercely rail;

When at the Doorga Poojah,
    And through the Bukree Eed,
The priests tell tales of heroes
    Renown'd in Eastern creed ;
When the woman cooks the curry,
    And piles it on the rice ;
And the baboo and the labourer
    Alike count up their pice,—
In every home in Agra,
    In many a place afar,
They'll tell the tale of that day when
    Jan Larrens held Durbar.

PARADISE AND THE PEELER.

When the Eden Gardens in Calcutta had been altered and very
much improved and were about to be thrown open to the public,
the Commissioner of Police issued an order that no one should be
admitted without a pass to be signed by himself, and he reserved to
himself the liberty of withdrawing any such pass without stating any
reason for so doing. The public were furious at this, and protests
and letters appeared daily in the papers, but it was reserved for this
squib to be the last feather that broke the camel's back. On the day
on which this squib appeared in the *Englishman* the obnoxious order
was withdrawn.

One eve a Peeler at the gate
Of Eden stood disconsolate;
And, as he listen'd to the band,
    Which play'd within, the music flowing,
In strains of his own native land,
    That set his Bobby's heart a-glowing,
He wept to think our out-cast race
Should be debarr'd that glorious place!

" How happy !" he sigh'd with a weary air,
" Are the two or three swells who wander there,

'Mid flowers whose scent can never pall!
Though mine are the haunts of Bow Bazaar
From Tank Square East to Sealdah far,
  This Garden of Eden is better than all!
Though bright are the rays which o'er Gunga gleam,
And pleasant in dinghees to go with the stream,
  And pleasant to ride without getting a fall,
Or to drive up and down until close of day,
'Mid yon swarm of buggies and carriages gay,
But—oh! 'tis only the swells can say—
  That a walk through Eden is better than all!

" Go, stroll around the cricket-ground there,
Or wander with ayahs about Tank Square,
  Or smoke a *dudeen* in the old Town Hall;
Of all the pleasures we find out here,
Our strolls with ayahs, our pipes, our beer,
  A half-hour in Eden is worth them all!"

The Great Chief who the key is keeping
Of Eden—saw the Peeler weeping,
And turn'd at once from off the course
And, drawing near, rein'd up his horse—
" Bobby!" he said, " I see thee cry,
Tell me at once the reason why!"

The Peeler wiping away a tear
With his cuff, replied, " My grief is clear;
No one but swells can enter here."
Then said the Chief " I'll soothe thy grief
And to thy bosom bring relief,
'Tis written, Bobby, by the Great
   That all to enter here are free
Who show the Peeler at the gate
   A pass or ticket sign'd by ME !"

Next day a gathering crowd appear'd
   Where Hogg, the Chief of Swelldom, reigns,
And sought from him they all revered
   A pass to Eden's sweet domains.
And as they ranged in muster by
Hogg scann'd them with Vice-regal eye.

A British merchant was the first
   Who stood before that searching gaze,
He seem'd as though with wealth he'd burst,
   Nor fear'd of Hogg's keen eye the blaze.
From Glasgow's crowded mart he came,
   And, through a long and bright career,
Had ever borne an honest name—
   A name full honor'd far and near,

Paradise and the Peeler.

"Sweet," said the Chief, "it is to stand,
   Renown'd for honor and for wealth ;
And sweeter 'tis to know we're loved
   For kindly actions done by stealth !
But still—alas !—the silver bar
Of Eden moves not,—worthier far
Than ev'n this merchant prince must be
The man who wants a pass from me !"

The merchant pass'd with piteous moan
That would have moved a heart of stone ;
And on his heels a lawyer came,
Dundreary should have been his name.
So long and full his whiskers red,
Which all around a halo shed,
His hat on one side of his head ;
A startling tie above his vest ;
A fresh-pluck'd rose upon his breast—
A spruce young spark was he who came
After the man of merchant fame,
And—'tis a dreadful thing to think,
He greeted Hogg with cheerful wink !

" Pass on ! pass on ! To none like you
   Can gates of Paradise open'd be,

The lawyer and the grasping Jew,
We class with Moslem and Hindoo,
    Who ne'er may Eden hope to see ;
Then ne'er need lawyer try to get
A ticket or a pass from me :"

Next came a broker calm and cool,
A courteous swell of the olden school,
So undisturb'd by care or glee,
The coolest card on earth is he ;
Well known to all the suppliants there,
He bow'd with calm collected air,
And coolly met Hogg's curious stare,
But, ah ! even brokers' hopes are vain,
Again the Chief forbade—again
Was Eden's barrier closed—" Not yet,"
The great Chief said, " with much regret,
From brokers I withhold the pass,
They're not in my Exclusive Class."

" Poor race of men !" said the pitying Bobby,
" Dearly ye pay for your new King Log,
Schalch ne'er would have yielded to any such hobby,
But the trail of the Service is all over Hogg !"

A tradesman next, who twenty years
   Had toil'd, and put his money by,
And made his shop a grand Hotel,
   And started a great Company—
Then to his native land retired
   And hoped to live in comfort there,
But times grew bad, and out he came
   The burden of these days to bear.
With him a sailor captain stood,
   Link'd with the tradesman, arm in arm,
Both bow'd and scraped in pleasant mood,
   And for their pass felt no alarm.
A civil engineer came next,
   A doctor, with no army rank,
An artist, and photographer,
   A chairman of a People's Bank—

" Nor tradesman rich, nor engineer,
   Nor sailor bold, nor artist smart,
Nor banker can get tickets here,
   I pray you then, my friends—depart !
The only people I can trust,
   And who in Eden wish to be,
Are leaders of the upper crust,
   And none but them I care to see—
For Eden's Gardens must be free
   From aught like doubtful company."

These gone, a dusky bride stood there,
With orange blossoms in her hair,
Pressing the arm of young Chee-Chee,
While, dress'd like her, were bridesmaids three—
Ah ! once how little Hogg did think
That from such sparkling eyes he'd shrink ;
That he would turn away his face
From sweet Eurasian form of grace ;
Turn from a bride of that swart race,
Whose dusky arms—whose fond grimace,
   Should gain as much respect from him
As priest from Israel's holiest place
   Could shew for Jewish Sanhedrim !

" Oh ! let us only breathe the air,
   The blessed air that's breathed by thee,
And let us wander blithely there
   Through Eden's Gardens for a spree—
Oh ! turn not from us thus your face,
   But tell us what we have to pay,
For well thou knowest we go the pace,
   And shell out on our wedding day."
Stern was the answer that he gave :
" To Chee-Chee charms I am no slave,
Like those who have already gone,
My powder'd friends, you must move on !"

But, hark—a pleasant sound is heard,
  The rustling of a satin dress,
As from her brougham steps a dame
  Bewitching in her loveliness—
With wreath'd smiles upon her face,
  And a gay twinkle in her eye,
Before the Chief she takes her place
  But thus to her he makes reply—
"When first you came into the room
  I knew you for that lady-bird,
Who lives alone and keeps a brougham—
  To let *you* in would be absurd.
The gates of Eden still are closed,
  Nor raised the silver bar can be,
How couldst thou, lady, have supposed
  Those gates I'd open, even for thee?"

And thus the crowd pass'd on afar,
  And fast the hours of daylight flew,
Not once was raised the silver bar,
  For none in all the crowd would do—
They all pass'd on ; Hogg could not bear
  To let them joys of Eden share.

" Poor race of men !" again sigh'd the Peeler,
    " Dearly ye pay for your new King Log,
In liberal notions Schalch was a dealer,
    But the trail of the Service is all over Hogg !"

What sudden sight disturbs the Chief,
    Why jumps he with convulsive start?
He sees to his intense relief
    An officer in war-paint smart !

" Oh ! glorious Lobster, come to me !
The silver bar is raised for thee—
For thee are opened Eden's gates,
For thee the Band in Eden waits.
What though of morals thou hast none,
Of wicked sire immoral son,
What though of all good thou art reft,
The Queen's commission thou hast left ;—
That uniform's enough for me,
And you, my Lobster brave, shall be
Through Eden's groves a wanderer free."

Another start and now appears
A Civil Servant, young in years,

But in his private life so loose,
And in his brains so sad a goose,
The ladies on that very score
Delight to pet him more and more.

" Oh! Haileybury boy! come here ;
For you and I school-fellows are,
To you shall Eden's path be clear,
For you is raised the silver bar."

(Chorus by Civil Servant and Lobster as they walk out of the Presence.)

Joy, joy, for ever! our task is done!
Hogg's pass is gain'd and Eden is won!
Oh! are we not happy? We are, we are!
To thee, sweet Eden, how dark appear
The dirty gullies of Jaun Bazar
And the evening pleasures we meet with there!

Farewell! ye snobs of earth, who ride
Upon the old Course after five,
Or creep along the river's side
Through what you call your evening drive!

Farewell! ye poor plebeian swells,
   Who gather in crowds along the strand,
Oh! what are the brightest joys you've known
Compared to ours when all alone
   We roam through Eden's flowery land?
Joy, joy, for ever! our task is done!
We've got Hogg's pass, and Eden is won!

THE VICE-REGAL FANCY-BALL.

January, 1866.

A RETROSPECT.

" She look'd so lovely as she sway'd
  Her partner with her finger-tips,
A man had given all other bliss
And all his worldly hopes for this,
To waste his whole heart in one kiss
  Upon her perfect lips—"
          —Slightly changed from Tennyson.

Come, let's recall the Fancy Ball of fifteen months ago,
When the upper crust of this great place made such a
      goodly shew;
When satin, silk, and velvet, and gold and silver sheen
Transform'd our dull Vice-regal halls into a fairy scene.

You well remember how you went, with long and flow-
      ing hair,
In costume that might well have done for Haidee or
      Gulnare;

A 1

No painter's brush could color, nor Grecian chisel trace,
A more becoming costume, a more bewitching face.

But, as to me, I felt at sea, for you had said that night,
When shewing off my uniform I look'd "a dreadful
    fright,"
Till then I always had supposed, though somewhat in
    the sere,
That I look'd well in war-paint as a gallant Volunteer.

But to the ball : who laughing came and walk'd you
    off apace ?
A well dress'd swaggering bold Zouave with kindly
    beaming face,
'Twas Monty, my old chum and friend, who ever
    plays the part,
Like his own Arab " Hermit," of thorough-bred at heart.

Now let me call to mind the throng that pass'd before
    me there,
And first (for some one must be first) the pretty
    Jardinière,
Who made her curtsey gracefully before the Viceroy's
    throne
With him who not long after call'd that Jardinière
    his own.

Then came a fair and comely dame with gorgeous
    train and dress,
And well she look'd and play'd her part of England's
    good Queen Bess;
Then "shorn and shaven" came a monk, with cowl
    and sandall'd feet,
Then lurid Mephistophiles—but where was Marguerite?

Now comes that clever horseman—I dare not mention
    names,
And if I did I'd only say his name was not *Fitz*-James ;
The Staff Corps' scarlet coat he wore, and, leaning
    on his arm,
A pretty wife clung to him with eyes of wondrous charm.

Pass on, my pretty lady, your eyes, all know full well,
Would work on those who gazed too long a too entran-
    cing spell :
Pass on, another takes your place, a heroine of Lucknow,
Who in the garb of Queen of Scots to England makes
    her bow,

And on her gentle face recalls those months of long
    despair,
When nothing but the cannon's roar was heard upon
    the air,

When life seem'd scarce worth living for, when blood
    ran cold from fright,
When sleepless night seem'd worse than day, and day
    seem'd worse than night.

Pass on, my English heroine, and take your sister too,
May she be spared the fearful scenes so well sustain'd
    by you;
Make room for this bold plunger with clanking sword
    and spur,
Who comes with Russian peasant girl envelop'd round
    with fur.

Bless us and save us! who are these? two elfs from
    Fairyland—
White hair, white wings, white dresses, white wands in
    either hand;
Pass on, pass on, those wings of your's were never
    meant to soar,
You'll find some day that love has wings to fly and
    come no more.

Doff your plumed hat, Lord Rochester, bend low your
    curly pate,
You're certainly a swell to-night, unconscious of the fate

Which waits the Bank of India in the crisis soon to
    come,
When you and other banker friends will have a run
    at home.

Zouave Vivandière passes on and makes her graceful
    bow,
A happy wife was she that night, a lonely widow now.
Then comes a learned LL.D., his sister by his side,
Who, as all pretty girls should do, has since become a
    bride.

Another Queen of Scots appears, two daughters in her
    train,
The one a comely Spaniard, the other " Lady Jane."—
Then an Italian brigand comes with murderous look
    and air
With a lady of the olden time with ruff and powder'd
    hair.

Ah me, here are two " powder'd-hairs," two pretty
    girls indeed,
Who with their beauty well might shake the Moslem
    Prophet's creed,

That houris are not found on earth, but as rewards are
    given,
To share eternal life with men who win their way to
    Heaven.

Pass on, you handsome specimens of England's powder'd
    hair,
Your stately mother well may think you fairest of the
    fair ;
Make way for that big Highlander, and for the mild
    Hindoo
Who smiles with dusky lips upon the daughter of a Jew.

Ah, pretty Lady Alice, if Amy Robsart were,
When Leicester's proud Earl loved her, but only half
    as fair
As you have made yourself to-night, no wonder he
    should rave
Through long remorseful years of grief o'er murder'd
    Amy's grave.

Now Pavia's Francis passes by dress'd out in gorge-
    ous style,
With a pretty little daughter of burning Sappho's isle,
A Corsair with Red-Riding-Hood, a Turco with Undine,
Her loose hair falling to her waist, in one light robe
    of green.

What " Snow" in this hot latitude? Ah, now a wail-
 ing cry
Seems ringing in my ears as when it rang from earth
 to sky,
When from the wreck on New Year's Day so many
 sought the shore,
And sank, like " Snow," beneath the tide to rise again
 no more.

" Hye-yah, chin-chin, fine pigeon-dress, hye-yah, my
 Mandarin,
The sun's your brother, moon your sister, stars your
 sons, chin-chin !
Pass on, my pig-tail'd friend, pass on, and join green
 Undine there,
And gaze upon the tangled tresses of Neœra's hair."

Ah, who is this tall Spanish girl, a daughter of the
 Church ?
For comelier form, for brighter eyes, 'twould take full
 long to search ;
My bright-eyed laughing maiden, what would not mor-
 tal dare
To take from you as pledge of love that rose-bud in your
 hair.

And now the gallant Highland Band the Night-bell
    Galop plays,
And crowds of dancers mingling there whirl through
    the giddy maze,
There kings and queens of classic days and of the olden
    time
Are galopping at such a pace as though to halt were
    crime.

There scarlet Mephistophiles tears round with white
    Undine
And bumps against a Scottish laird with Hungary's fair
    queen;
And "Effie Deans" is very nearly lifted off her feet
By the frantic rush of Turco whirling round with
    Marguerite.

But waltz soon follows galop, and then a staid quad-
    rille
In which I have as partner my Maiden of Castille;
And when tis o'er Friar Tuck comes up with "Night"
    upon his arm,
And whispers thus, "The champagne's good, a glass
    won't do you harm."

I take the hint—come back—and find that all with
    powder'd hair
Have form'd a Louis Quinze Quadrille which no one else
    may share ;
All other dancers gather round to watch the dancers
    here,
And what a handsome set they are, each Dame and
    Cavalier.

There where the eyes are brightest her bright dark eyes
    are seen,
Whose graceful form and lovely face might stamp her
    Beauty's Queen :
That graceful form, those winning ways, will now for
    many a year
Assert their reign o'er all her guests who flock to
    Belvidere.

But neither time nor space allows to dwell on ' powder'd
    hair,'
It is enough for me to say that all were handsome
    there ;
And many a throbbing heart will find its memory
    haunted still
By beaming eyes which sparkled from that Louis Quinze
    Quadrille.

Now plumed hat, and gold-and-green, and purple, pink,
    and buff,
And blue-and-silver, high-heel'd shoes, short waist, and
    lace, and ruff
Have mix'd again with Turk, Zouave, Undine, Paysanne,
    Francaise,
Corsair, Vivandière, good Queen Bess, Greek girl, and
    Polonaise.

And so the revelry went on—my brain was in a whirl,
I chatted now with Scottish lass, then with a flower
    girl ;
I took to supper Maid of Spain, pull'd bon-bons with
    Undine,
And drank a glass of sparkling hock with Shakespeare's
    Fairy Queen.

But all the while I thought as now I think of that gay
    ball,
You were, my little petted wife, the prettiest of them
    all ;
I told you so when home we came, I tell you so to-day,
To me you were the prettiest there, whatever others say.